# I Hate Junk Food

# I Hate Junk Food
## A satire and other short pieces
## Dirk Holger

## Translated by Tina Maloney

THE Beckham
PUBLICATIONS GROUP, INC.

**Silver Spring**

Published in the United States by
Beckham Publications Group, Inc.
ISBN: 0-931761-88-3
10 9 8 7 6 5 4 3 2 1

To My American Family

# Contents

# Preface

Any idiot can write a book, but not everyone who is borderline literate can write a book that is enthusiastically welcomed by the reader. Anyone can hear the birds chirping, but who can apply meaning to their songs? Only very few (the "chosen ones," perhaps?) are as naïve as Siegfried or perhaps St. Francis, who actually heard the birds talk. I believe I'm among those chosen few, and I have good reason to believe so. Many years ago did not a little sparrow whisper to me from the shingled roof of our abode,

"Create order out of chaos. Commit your random notes to paper. Set a deadline and stick to it—write a book!"

Oh boy. Fool that I am, I actually listened to the silly bird, sat down, and without question (albeit not without contemplation) started the monumental task of transforming the countless little "notes" I had scribbled onto any suitable material in the most unlikely places into "something" literary.

Very early one morning, while the kids were asleep, I began to feed my "collection" into the typewriter. By then, the sparrow had fallen prey to an owl and, on the very same morning, the very same owl passed by my open window, and stared at me with her owl eyes.

"Be careful! Think about what you are doing," she cried out to me.

I'm serious. For a split second, I even thought I heard the voice of the sparrow coming from the owl's beak. Thus, I began to contemplate what I was about to do.

This contemplation lasted a long time. After three years had passed without any messages from chirping birds, I threw the owl's caution to the wind, or rather, placed it on the back burner of my consciousness. I sat down once again to peck at the typewriter keys, this time with a little more force and confidence. By the time I had reached the ripe old age of 61, I had some results—the very book you are holding in your hands right now, dear reader.

Doesn't every writer wonder prior to publication whether it is all "worth it," whether the reader will actually accept the product of many nights of feverish typing? Not I! I simply kept on writing. Did it make "sense" to transform the collection of little loose notes into printed form? I will leave the answer up to you, dear reader. If you are bored, I will provide you with a refund of your money, or a knock in the head; the choice is entirely mine. All kidding aside, though, the question remains whether I would have ever written a book if it had not been for the chirping of birds.

Well, I've never experienced a lack of ideas for smart-aleck phrases with which to put my jumpy thought processes into words. Perhaps this book is even a symbol of my "coming of age."

My esteemed Latin professor, Dr. Heinrich Hahne (1911-1996), who will frequently cross the reader's path in my stories, told me back in preparatory school in Wuppertal, Germany: "Dirk, you can go to bed with a top hat on, and you'll still never be a gentleman." He was right, of course. I never achieved nobility, nor did I ever become a gentleman. But I did "grow up," and in this, my 62nd year, it is about time. I hope that those of you who already know me, and those of you who will get to know me through this book, will accept this labor of love as a sign of my coming of age at a time when my contemporaries have already retired and are living happily on their pensions. God willing, I am not planning on doing any such thing prior to my 90th birthday, if at all. So go ahead, turn off the blaring television and turn on your reading light. I'm about to share with you a piece of my fertile mind.

# AMERICAN TALES

# The Lost Sheep

Quite some time has passed since I was a city bird, a night owl residing as an alien resident from farther up north in the vicinity of Washington, DC. Of my many strange encounters there (and they were all strange) on my nightly hunt for rats (that city is full of them), I recall only two or three that still bring a smile to my beak. My other experiences were, in one word, disastrous. Here is one of the happy events of my "high and low life" in this famous (for what?) capital.

One midsummer night—near dawn, that is—I was perched on a high branch of a linden tree so big a regular street light underneath it looked like a small toy from where I perched. As you all may know, I need no light; my eyes are actually better in the dark. What did I see there? What did I hear?

A swaying, shadowy figure lingered along an alley near my hideout and it was sort of singing. It could not have been a rat since it was far too big, and rats don't sing—or do they in DC? Finally, I could make out this ghostly figure: it was one of you humans. I must say that I am well versed in Bible verses since my home tree stands near a black church of the highest order. That night I learned a few more.

It was an elegantly dressed black man staggering down the dark alley. When he reaches the light post he holds onto it in such a way that I can tell he is inebriated, a "wino," as you humans call someone who drinks too much, too often. He is carrying an old leather-bound Bible, how wonderful. But no, he has a flask stashed inside it and takes a drink from it—out of the Bible, it appears. What is this world coming to?

I hear him clearly, reading from his liquor Bible. "Save me, O Lord, from the hands of the wicked. Preserve me (hic) from violent men who plan to... to... to... trip my feet. By the wayside they have laid (hic) snares for me!"

He flips through his "Bible" and takes a drink.

"If a man pushes another out of hatred (hic), or after laying in wait for him, throws something at him and causes his... his death; or if he strikes another out of enmity [Out of what?] and causes his death, he shall be put to death as a... a murderer. The avenger of blood may ex... ex... execute the murderer on... sight (hic). Great justice!"

In the dark behind him, another figure sneaks up. It is a sneak, not a walk; it looks dangerous. How can I warn the wino of what I see? What to do? Alarm! The stranger has a big knife and puts it into the pocket of his large, baggy pants. It is a young white man approaching the wino in a threatening way. He circles the old, preaching black man and tries to keep in the shadows. Could it be that this self-made preacher is a soothsayer? His Bible verses refer directly to the situation he is in right now. How should I warn him? I start to sound my famous, eerie "hoot, hoot," but to no avail. He believes that he himself is producing the sound of an owl. Maybe he is hooting down his inner voice that is trying to tell him that danger is near; maybe... How can this poor man, who is dressed so well and looks so clean and must have come from a good home, how can he drink out of a Bible, I ask you? He does it again and pays no attention to the stranger sneaking up behind him.

"For I shall suffer it if a man enslaves me, if a man de... de... de... devours me, if a man takes from me, if a man sl... slaps my face. Hallelujah!"

At that very moment, the stranger enters the circle of light cast by the street lamp, steps quickly in front of the Bible lover.

"Hands up! Give me everything!"

The wino is surprised and asks, "Are you drunk?"

Confused, the stranger-turned-mugger stutters, "Am I what? No, I'm hungry you... you drunkard. Wait, what's this? I ask the questions, not you. Give me your money, right now!"

What does our tipsy preacher do? He spreads his arms wide and calls happily, "Come to Jesus! Then you will... will... will... will...not need money" (hic).

Furious, the mugger slaps him. "There's your Jesus! And here... and here! You... you drunk! I'll give you a Jesus. Here! There!"

As the wino protects himself from the beating with his Bible, he mutters, "Oh, no, do... do... do... do... don't hit me, honey." He still appears not to be scared by the stranger.

The mugger tries to pick his pockets, knowing that he has a defenseless victim in front of him. "What? I'm not your honey." He draws the knife out of his pocket and pokes at the wino. "Your money! Now!"

I almost fall off my tree branch when I hear the wino giggle, "Kill me (hic), torture me, slaughter me (hic), but... but... but don't tickle me! Please, never tickle me." He quotes again, "The day of the Lord is near in the valley of destruction..."

To which the mugger responds: "I see no... valley. This is an alley, not a valley, you preaching ox"—and this said with a glower on his face.

His grim expression changes to amusement when the wino continues, "Your deeds shall be avenged sevenfold. And if you tickle me once more (hic) ... seven times sevenfold."

The bemused mugger says: "Funny man, eh?"

Still giggling, the wino is unaware of the immediate threat. "Jesus, how funny."

The wino flips through his Bible. "If someone lies in wait for his (hic) neighbor out of hatred for him and rising up against him, strikes him mortally and then (hic) what?"

Cutting him short, the mugger yells, "I don't hate you, man. All I want is your money, 'cause I need it, you hear me?"

Again he threatens him with the knife and cannot believe his ears as the wino continues.

"Blessed be the penniless man, for his (hic) is ..."

Infuriated, the mugger circles him. "Cut your stupid salvation sermon. What are you, a soused apostle or something?" The wino keeps on.

"I live for the ho… holy word and share all I have with the… the poor (hic). Listen to what the Bible says: 'I was not sent except for the lo… lo… lo… lost sheep. You are that lost sheep. But (hic) such knowledge is not in everyone (hic)."

I ask myself, is he deaf or fearless? He could be killed by that man. Now the mugger has had it and he attacks the helpless (but not hopeless) wino.

"You got no money? Not you. You share with the poor, you said? Well, I'm poor, share! What's in that book? You're hiding something in that Bible. What is it? Give me that book, or else!"

The wino refuses. In the ensuing struggle the flask slides out of the Bible, falls to the ground, and shatters into many pieces that scatter all over the alley. I see the stranger retreat, jumping away from the splashing whiskey. The wino's words call him back.

"Can you read?" The Bible is firmly held in the black man's outstretched hands.

Totally perplexed, the mugger retorts, "Can I what?"

"Can you (hic) re… read?"

This drives the mugger mad. "Shut up! That book! If you can hide a whole flask of booze in it, you can hide money in it, too. I can tell. Give me that book now!"

He pushes the man again and the wino giggles even more. "You are too much. Can't read… and de … de … desires to read my holy book? Oh, I know."

"Who knows? Who knows what, damn it? Tell me!" Now the mugger pokes at him more with his knife.

Not feeling frightened, the wino says, "God alone knows. And He holds His hands over the ho… holy… and the (hic) …"

The mugger cannot help but laugh at this and tickles him even more.

"You? Holy? You? You black mourner at your own funeral. Here, and there." By now highly amused, he makes the poor wino dizzy by dancing around him.

"Stop that, you idiot. (hic) Stop piercing me or I'll clobber you," the wino cries out. Then he uses some more well chosen Bible verses which, unfortunately, my little owl brain forgot. They cause the mugger to ponder his aggravation.

As you, dear reader, surely belong to the strong believers in the power of the Holy Word, you must be highly pleased to witness the miraculous way it works here, as the mugger seems to be no longer a threat to our street preacher and ... What is that? Oh no, what does my owlish eyes see?

The mugger is not so much amused as angered by the drunken man's never-ending sermon. He throws himself, knife in hand, at the surprised wino, who raises both his arms high up and then it happens... He hits the mugger over the head with his Bible. The mugger staggers and falls to the ground. The wino is jubilant.

"This is my sweet-smelling oblation to the Lord. There you have it, you ... you white bastard." He looks down in total surprise and cannot figure out why the mugger does not get up, so he talks down to him.

"Oh, what are you doing in the dir ... dirty street? Get up, honey, get up! I'm sorry, please get up! I didn't mean to knock ... knock you out, no, not me."

He stares at his empty Bible and fishes another flask out of his jacket pocket, drinks, and explains.

"You see, this holy book holds a hidden power. It's Jesus' power, not mine (hic). Jesus knocked you out." He then counts to ten like a referee in a boxing ring. "That's it, poor man, get up! You are for ... forgiven. I'll read you a line or two from the holy script. To you, you stupid, can't read and want my book, can't even count. I said, ten. Get up, dummy, or you'll be damned for all eternity. Listen! Thou shalt not ..."

Suddenly, the mugger gets up, enraged, and tries to run his knife into the wino, crying, "Enough is enough."

At that very moment, the siren of an approaching police car can be heard. The mugger runs away.

Not realizing that the threat is gone, the wino intonates blissfully again, "Thou shalt not (hic) kill. Thou shalt not mug, not slaughter, (hic) not torture, and not tickle. Thou shalt not murder." As he finds himself alone, he calls out after the mugger.

"Where are you, brother? Come back! Come mug me! O Lord, forgive him, for having tickled me. Amen." As he slowly walks away, the police siren subsides.

He must be reading his Bible again. "Draw near to God and he will (hic) draw near to you. Cleanse your hands, all you sinners and purify your hearts, you double. ...double-minded (hic). Be sorrowful and weep ... and weep ... and weep. Oh, I said that. And your laughter be turned into mourning (hic) and your joy into sadness. Humble yourselves in the sight of the Lord and he will... exalt you."

From here on, I hear his voice only as a faint mumbling.

"Confess, therefore, your sins to one another (hic) and pray for one another ... that you may be saved ... you ...all."

I almost fell off my branch again when I heard him loudly yell, "Hallelujah!" What a night. I took off after the rats!

# "Talk, Tree, Talk!"
## In Memoriam—Jane Pittman

*[An interrupted monologue for Beola, a black lady over 100 years old and the voice of an old tree (on tape). The setting: a bench under the tree, a mighty oak.*
*The time: the present]*

[Beola deliberately approaches the tree and looks around several times, as though someone is following her, and as though she is talking to someone...]

### BEOLA

And this here old oak, no he doesn't talk to just anyone, you know, not just anyone. *(She sits down carefully and leans against the tree trunk, which she occasionally strokes, speaking to it and to an unseen person in the distance)* See, this old tree talks to me, and I talk to him, as often as I want or whenever he wants to. Whenever I talk to my friend the tree, I sit down and make myself nice and comfortable, so comfortable that I have sat here for so many hours, day after day, for oh-so-many years. Now I'm old, real old, and too tired to do a lot of talking when I talk with him. But I still have a deep respect for him, a lot of respect just like I know he has for me. I have my life behind me. I've always shared my happy days and sad days with my oak, which has been growing old with me. Do you know I'm going to be one hundred and three years old tomorrow? But my friend the tree is much, much older than me. What is time to him? Nothing. I have always understood what he has had to say for so many, many years gone by, always. We get along like two good old friends, my tree and I. You must know, my tree talks to me in a deep, tender voice, barely audible. He certainly doesn't speak to just anybody, he wouldn't listen to just anybody, either. He decided on me, and so I am the only one who hears his voice. He's Mother Nature to me. See, I can understand how other people can't hear him, but I hear him when everything is silent—totally silent. When ... *(she pauses and closes her eyes)*

## TREE

Beola, stay awake. Please keep talking to me. You can't fall asleep now. Your heartbeat is getting slower, I can feel it—wake up!

## BEOLA

Thank you, dear tree, thank you. *(She smiles.)* I already know what you want to tell me. I've been thinking it for a long time. My old heart is beating slower in the last seventy, eighty years, but it hasn't stopped beating—not yet. In the last two, three years it's gotten a lot older, more tired than in the hundred years before. Now it beats so slowly. I can walk once all the way around your trunk before the second heartbeat and before you hear the third one, someone could have had a baby, brought it up, taken it to kindergarten. No, I'm exaggerating. I take it back... but... to come with the child out of the shadows into a light that... You see? A short path into the brightness... that's what I mean, and, before you've counted to four my one hundred and third birthday will be celebrated by nobody, alone, peaceful here with you. Time? It doesn't fly, it doesn't run away, it is just flowing over me, don't you think so, too?

## TREE

I believe you.

## BEOLA

You see, you know me. Not even a birthday party with a birthday cake would make my heart beat faster, or want to pick up time. You become more serene when you're as old as I am, and still I know how young I am compared to you with your over eight hundred proud years, as they say.

## TREE

Eight hundred ninety-eight, Beola.

## BEOLA

Yes, yes, you just keep on counting upwards ... and me? I count down. God, to think how young we both were when we talked to each other for the first time...

## TREE

I remember it very well, Beola. You had just turned fifty-seven and I was a solid eight hundred fifty-two years old, or young, in your way of counting time. A beautiful, warm, sunny day it was, but you were going to tell me something else?

## BEOLA

You are my conscience and consciousness, my friend. *(She breathes deeply)* I wanted to tell you I ... I forgot. See? That's what we people call senile. Trees don't know it; how nice. Time? It trickles, hurries, parts, lingers, heals, and I don't even know how old the other trees around us are...

## TREE

I know their ages, all of them. But what about your birthday, Beola?

## BEOLA

My dear, old oak tree, I've stopped counting from one year to the next. I just don't have the time. Funny, isn't it? Once you get so old, then you celebrate every dawn. Every new day seems to be a gift from heaven. Every hour is a mercy. I breathe time in with every breath. I breathe deeply and consciously and I look at the world, you, still a strange world where I am not at home. Early in the morning I hear an unknown bird singing from afar, very far away, like from another world. I get up slowly, shuffle across the garden here to you, to be with you and no one else. I sit down here on our bench, here under this canopy of leaves and when I am so close to you, my wise old oak, then I believe I am closer to my God and can hear His heart beating through you. *(She sighs deeply again, relieved.)* Time needs time and I need you. I'm sure you still have a lot to say and I would, I could listen to you for a long time still if I weren't so tired. *(She falls asleep.)*

## TREE

Beola! Beola, wake up. Don't fall asleep on me now!

## BEOLA *(wakes up)*

Thank you—oh, my goodness! I can hear you. Only you know what is good *(as if to herself)*. How strange. No one has ever asked whether my old tree has anything like an intelligence, or a soul, or wit. No one asked whether my speaking with him, or his listening has another, unknown, deeper source. Which? This is, and will always be, my last question. So. And there I've said it. *(She pauses and turns back towards the tree.)* My dear, old, loyal tree! To think of all the things you have experienced, how many fates, atrocities, how much injustice, hate, and enmity, how much unhappiness you must have seen... but still you bloom, still your leaves are green, and still you give me shade. You have been the witness to so much human suffering, degradation, crime, everything woven into your dark-green dreams, which will burst forth so that everywhere in the grieving world every reason for joy or hope is washed away with streams of tears, year in and year out, endless, tears dropping from your leaves and from your branches ... and wars and slaughter and the lust for war rampage on—rampage still. This earth is a stage of terror for fear, disaster for so many innocent souls who are buried by time—so much death. And still you grow, and stand strong and tall and firm in the wind and in the most terrible storms, and you protect my old wooden bench and you protect me, for how long yet?

## TREE

You amaze and astound me again and again, Beola.

## BEOLA

Again and again? All things that have time are fascinating, but things that stand above time, the cycles of the universe, are even more exciting, you know. They stand outside of time. No rhythm of the natural world could equal these infinitely large supernatural cycles and we seem so tiny before them, so small. All living things are only a metaphor; at least that's how I see it. The world stands above all iniquity, above it's own hell that it holds, and it stays holy. I touch you *(she does so)* and through you I touch the other world, outside of us. And then again, in my dreams, I am in the other world and I'm even closer to you there, a riddle, to be close to both worlds, to be without time. But this small fleck on the great wide world is my paradise; I don't need a hereafter. This place under my old oak belongs to me, otherwise I have nothing, and I desire nothing else. Here is where I want to rest... when no more tears come into my eyes. Here.

### TREE

Today you are comforting me with your words, Beola. Don't you still have something special to say to me?

### BEOLA

Oh, I don't know. I'm probably just less silly than I am other days. I don't have much, I don't have anything more to say. I have lived. Do you know that Oracle? 'Behind every blue horizon sleeps a deep darkness that just waits to be awakened in us.' Strange, isn't it?

### TREE

And I honestly believed you were going to answer me.

### BEOLA

I am. But, what is an answer anyway? Nothing, or not everything, is worth an answer. What did you ask me? I've already forgotten. I'm so terribly tired today. So, we waste a few thoughts on life, in life, and then we fall silent and life passes us by, and we hardly become aware why ... *(She falls into a deep sleep ... for always.)*

## TREE

Don't worry about the questions. Life itself is the question. Beola! Hello! I can hardly hear your heartbeat anymore. It's getting weaker, ever weaker. Beola, wake up! Beola, don't leave me. Stay with me… my only friend, my only soul mate, you my own. May heaven bless you.

*(It quickly becomes dark.)*

# Sunset in Olney

I used to be a city owl. But I flew out of the "District," north-northwest, and landed near a place called something like "Olney," a town in Maryland that is still fairly heavily forested (though not for long). There is a square there at the edge of a forest from which you can see very far. On the square is a beautiful old maple tree with a bench beside it. It must have been placed there by a connoisseur of spectacular sunsets because its view to the west makes this place unique, especially on evenings near summer's end. On those evenings, as you sit on the bench and look to the west, it seems as though you are gazing into a sea of flames. There is an elderly married couple from Olney who loves the bench below the tree as much as I love the tree itself as a resting spot and as a starting point for my nightly hunting.

For days, I have been watching this couple, which call each other as "Winston" and "Theodora," come here, and I keep one eye closed, in case they arrive too early and disturb me in my daily sleep. They are both very talkative, constantly rattling on about God and the world and, their favorite topic, the peaceful atmosphere of this place, the silence that surrounds and engulfs them. The silence here at the edge of the forest would be about three times more wonderful if those two would just shut up. They just can't help sharing their views with anyone nearby, whether they want to hear or not. The memorable events of this particular evening were no different. Winston sits down first, after which he lets Theodora choose the best spot on the bench, because the sunset has already begun, and you get more out of it if you sit in the front row. They kiss each other gently and hold hands, like two young lovers. It's a joy to see them like this.

"Just look, Theodora," says Winston, "how beautifully the radiant sun bids farewell to this quiet day."

"And tomorrow, dear Winston, the sun will rise and shine for us again."

"Here in Olney," Winston replies with a contented smile.

"It is so peaceful out here, silent as the grave. I just love living in Maryland."

Winston nods. "Oh, yes. It was the calmness of this area that enticed us to spend our golden years here." He pauses for a moment, reflecting. "It's too bad we're so close to the District, with its rat race, political corruption, and all those terrible shootings every day."

Owls have sensitive ears, and I think I hear an undertone here. But Theodora smiles at Winston. "It's bad, yes. But we're at a safe distance out here, darling. Nothing could ever happen out here, nothing."

Naturally, I know their daily ritual of self-reassurance and would prefer to tune it out, but I can't. It's not as though they're whispering—they're probably talking so loudly because their old age has made them somewhat hard of hearing.

Winston scratches the back of his head and looks carefully at his wife. "Yesterday, I read an article in the paper—which is about 80 percent advertisements, by the way ..."

Theodora nods. "The *Washington Post.*"

"Let me finish. The article was about an old married couple like us—yes, it could have been us, Theodora—who were shot for no reason while sitting on their front porch on Third Street, Northeast. Some man with an NRA logo on his jacket passed by and killed them. Poor folks."

Theodora looks shocked. "How about that. What reason could he have possibly had to murder them?"

Winston sighs. "No reason, no meaning, just two people dead for the fun of shooting."

Theodora for a moment is sympathetic. "Terrible, just terrible. Or maybe it was fate. After all, when your time comes, your time comes. But, we are still alive and doing well. We'll live here for years to come. No one could harm us, no one would disturb the precious solitude we enjoy out here. Life has been good to us, Winston. Your life has enriched mine, and I thank God every day for having blessed us this way."

Winston embraces her. "You are my blessing, Theodora. Our lives are more or less fulfilled. Here we are, sharing the beauty of yet another sunset in Olney and... but ..."

Theodora looks concerned. "Yes? What?"

Looking very serious, Winston takes his arm from around her shoulder. "Nothing. That's all."

"You look so concerned all of a sudden, Winston."

He shakes his head. "It's nothing, dear."

Theodora is persistent. "There is something wrong, Winston. I can tell."

"Theodora, believe me," Winston says with great emphasis. "If I had to die today, right here next to you, I would not regret it. This is all I have lived and worked for. This, to watch with you, my love, the Indian summer sunsets at Olney."

Theodora is all ears. "No, you don't mean that, not really. You don't want to die. Are you telling me you have struggled all your life for this—peaceful place out here in our quiet corner of the earth? Is there nothing else you could envision; no wishes for the future?"

"Nothing dear, other than our tomorrow to be like our today, to be with you till the end. We are one, you and I. Never have I felt it more overwhelmingly than today, here on our wooden park bench in this fated spot."

Theodora stands up and examines the bench. "Our fated spot? Aren't you exaggerating a little?" She sits back down, having observed nothing unusual about the wooden bench.

Winston remains serious. "This is where our fate lies, whether you believe it or not. Here, not at home, is where I want to die at your side while watching the sunset."

Theodora regards him soberly. "You speak so seriously and solemnly. All I can say is Amen."

First, Winston looks high up into the tree, as though he is trying to discover me up here, then he looks at her and then back at the sunset burning on the horizon. "I sense an otherworldly, even divine, presence more intensely when we are spending our time together here at the edge of the forest. Don't you feel it, too?"

"Not when you're talking."

Is the woman absolutely heartless? I start listening intently because I thought I heard a sound in the bushes behind the tree, but now it's still again; I must have been wrong. But owl ears are never wrong.

Winston's voice is more solemn than I've ever heard it before. "Peacefulness is with the pious, the honest, the simple-hearted."

Theodora cuts him off. "The simple-minded."

"I'm including you, too, Theodora," he says without mockery. "In Olney ..."

"Well, who doesn't live peacefully here in Olney? In Olney we drive no streetcar named disaster, not here. No shooting, no killing, no sudden murders, no, no."

"Talk sense, woman. The things you say. We live in Maryland. We passed one of the toughest laws banning guns. A strong expression against those gun nuts on Sixteenth Street."

"No guns, no shooting. It's that simple!"

Winston shakes his head. "I could never live down there in that perpetual nastiness. They even try to further spread arms. Now the bullet-lovers are urging Congress to put machine guns in every American home. Sickening!"

Theodora is reflective as she answers. "If the NRA had an office in Olney, they would—"

"Would do what?" Winston asks with scorn, "supply all the kids with toy guns for early lessons, and adults with dueling pistols?"

"With whom would you duel out here?" Theodora asks dryly.

"We should praise the Lord that we don't have a mayor in our community smoking pot and ignoring all the street murders. It grates on me."

"What, Winston?"

"The thought that no one can stop those gun freaks from advocating today what might have made sense in the Eighteenth Century—the 'right to bear arms.' Don't you know Theodora what the NRA's final goal is: for each and every American to possess a deadly weapon. If possible, an armful in each home. Idiots like this senile Hollywood star drive me crazy with their 'freedom to carry arms' slogans. When you speak out against them, your own freedom of speech is shot at."

Theodora sighs. "Guns kill, any gun."

"After all," Winston adds, "guns are meant to be used. And they go on with their gun promotion and murder promotion. It's all one and the same."

Again I hear rustling in the underbrush near the tree, but don't see any mouse. I wasn't mistaken earlier. Quickly, I fly down a few branches.

"If I were forced to own a gun, Winston, I'd throw it away. Yes! I would even if a burglar broke into our house."

I hear a very quiet crunching noise, and it's coming closer and now I see a stranger sneaking up to the tree. As hard as my owl eyes try, I can't see what he's holding in his hand, something black. The elderly couple has eyes and ears only for each other.

"Don't worry yourself, Theodora," says Winston, "our dear old forest stands firm and green between us and that dirty, deadly city life. We hear birds singing, not ambulance sirens wailing. I look at the sky, this vast dome above us, and see God in his domicile."

Theodora corrects him. "God's house isn't in the sky, Winston. He lives in the church."

"In church? No, that's where he does his business." Winston pauses, clears his throat, and then continues. "No, God lives in heaven, from where he has a watchful eye on us and our community. No smog hinders him from seeing us clearly."

The two are silent for a moment, as though they had just heard a noise, even though they have never met another living soul out here. But the forest stays silent and Winston continues.

"By the way, my dear, where did you hide our valuables this time? I know you rotate our two treasure boxes twice a year. Why?"

"Three boxes, Winston."

Unbeknownst to the couple, a stranger has sneaked up behind the tree and is listening to their every word. What is he planning? The thought of a possible confrontation makes me uneasy. What should I do? I wait and listen.

"Why are there three boxes now?"

Theodora starts listing them off on her fingers. "One for my own jewels—"

"Which you never wear."

"One for Grandma's jewelry, the kind that every jewelry dealer dreams of—thank goodness we've never had to sell them—and one for your rare coin collection."

Winston seems a little resentful. "Why did you do that, without telling me? Where are they this time? I'm only asking because a burglar might not find them and would then become a murderer out of frustration. One of the boxes must be ready for sacrifice, but not mine, please."

"Don't worry, dear. I'll always be able to find my boxes."

"I insist. I want to know."

Theodora smiles. "You have your secrets, I have mine."

Winston actually seems angry. "No more games! Tell me where they are."

"If you'd just be polite and say 'please,' I'd tell you."

Winston sighs. "Please."

Theodora begins to reveal things that are not meant for other ears, but she knows nothing of the listener behind the tree.

"Well, if I remember correctly, the first box is inside the locker in the attic. It's all wrapped up in an old cloth. The second box with your coin collection is… in a rusty container, well stored away in the basement, labeled…"

"Clever, dear, very clever. Those are the first places a burglar would look, the basement and the attic. Well-hidden!

Nonsense. Remember, Theodora, those boxes contain our life insurance, but no burglar will ever visit us." "And the third box, with Grandma's elegant and pictorial ambers, gold, and other gems, some of them very old... I forgot that one. Sorry." "You better not forget, darling. They're very valuable. Try to remember."

"Well, Winston, if my little brain tells me correctly, they are all scattered throughout the house—and for good reason." "So they're not in the third box?"

"That was too unsafe. Yes, now I remember. I hid the ambers on top of Grandpa's clock, the gold necklaces are... in the blue pitcher in the kitchen cabinet, filled to the top with candies as camouflage, and small things such as the rings, diamonds are well hidden—piece by piece—behind the leather-bound books on the shelves in your room, dear." Winston can't believe his ears.

"You must be out of your mind—in my room, of all places. That's the most dangerous place you could choose, with the door to the garden. Any idiot would first look behind the books."

Theodora whispers something to Winston. "Speak up, woman," he grumbles. "No one is out here but us."

"See how the orange over there is changing to red? Golden rays are bathing our park ridge. The world is quiet now. Yes, what?"

"I'm not interested in the spectacle right now. Come to your senses, woman. Anyone with the intention of breaking into our home would first... by the way, where did you put the keys?"

Theodora continues, as though she doesn't hear him. "When our time has come and we haven't spent our valuables, we can generously give the rest to charity, don't you think?" "The keys!"

Theodora rummages in her dress. "Surprise! I brought them this time. Both of them—the key to the back door too. Besides, our house is the only one on this lonely country road."

Finally, Winston is reassured. "Good, I'm glad. You have brought gentleness into my life, Theodora. I will cherish this forever."

Theodora sighs contentedly, the little spat completely forgotten. "Of all the words you have said to me today, dearest, these last ones will make me happy even in my dreams."

Suddenly, the dusk's evening hues of red are gone and it is darker. Both of them are quiet for a while; the stranger behind the tree, too, is quiet. Until now, I really haven't paid him much attention. Maybe he really isn't a stranger to the old couple. But what will this dimming evening bring? In the ensuing silence, an indefinite feeling of danger emerges, an unseen threat. I hope that I am deceiving myself, silly owl that I am, and the evening's peace will bring the longer peace of night for those below. For me, it will bring my departure on my silent hunt for mice. The elderly lovers interrupt the silence.

Winston places his arm around his wife's shoulders and says in a tender voice, "Thank you for everything, for all the happiness you brought into my life, Theodora."

Her thoughts seem to be elsewhere. "See, Winston, old age does have its advantages. Ah, if only this old tree could speak and its leaves could sing."

Winston shakes his head. "Talk sense, woman."

Theodora's train of thought changes tracks yet again. "The two of us have really had it with the gun maniacs in the District, haven't we?"

"What brought this up?" Winston asks confused.

"Wasn't there a hunter living in Olney at the end of the last century? He had a parrot and shot him by mistake?"

Winston smiles indulgently. "That's another story, my dear. But you only know the end of this strange parrot's story. I'll tell you what really happened in 1877, or 1899, or 1888, it was some year where the last two digits were the same, wasn't it?"

"You're asking the wrong person. You made this all up, Winston. Or so I was told."

Curiously, I lean almost too far forward on my branch and barely catch myself in time. Any story involving a bird interests me. Incredulous, but confirmed by his words, the stranger in the shadows and I listen to Winston tell the following story.

"Listen carefully, Theodora. This is what occurred somewhere near where the Olney Theatre now stands, near the swampy thickets. There was a woodcutter who lived in a cottage in this, then, very remote area with his fourteen-year-old son. He was a widower for quite a while and raised his son in the middle of the forest all by himself. To help his little Micah overcome hours of loneliness at home while he worked in the woods, the woodcutter bought his son a parrot. Soon, this parrot—imported from some French-speaking island in the Caribbean—learned some words not meant for everyone's ears. He could leave his cage anytime he desired. He flew around the house in the morning, actually each morning, only to come back for food and for Micah's entertainment. To Micah's joy, the parrot would always come back to him and say things such as: 'Feed me, feed me' and other things only Micah knew."

"Isn't that sweet," says Theodora. "What a lovely story."

"It was the old man's habit to make himself a large sandwich each morning to eat for lunch in the forest. If he couldn't make it back home in time, he usually saved some of it for supper. On one of those long-gone days, he bit into his sandwich only to find that the butter was gone. He was sure he had spread butter on it. Well, the next morning, he spread twice the amount of butter on his bread and left for the woods. The parrot joined him for a short time and then flew off. At lunch time, when the woodcutter opened his basket the butter was gone again. This happened several days in a row and the woodcutter decided to keep a keen eye on both his basket and his son before leaving his home. Only little Micah could be playing this little game, he thought. Finally, he discovered this scene: each time after spreading the butter on his bread and placing it in his basket, he went to the pump outside his house. On that day, he hid behind the door watching through one of the many holes in the wood. With widening eyes, he saw that Micah was quietly eating his breakfast and was unaware of what was going on behind him. The parrot flew to the basket, opened it with his strong beak, and unfolded the bread with his legs, smeared the butter off the bread and all over his beak. He then placed the sandwich back together, closed the basket, and flew away. For many days, the woodcutter wondered why the parrot would steal his butter. He soon remembered that the parrot flew in the same direction every day. So he followed him."

"Where to?" asks Theodora. "Silver Spring? Rockville? The District? Germany?"

"Honey," sighs Winston. "Those first three places existed only as small dots on a map and Germany... why Germany? Germany didn't even exist as a unified nation back then, you know. Now, our parrot with his buttered beak flew straight to the ravine, right there in the forest."

"And then the parrot ate the butter, right?"

"Wrong. At the end of the ravine stood a large, shiny rock shaped like a slope, some ten to fifteen yards long. Here, the parrot walked slowly up the entire rock and spread the butter from his beak onto the rock. After smearing butter to the very top, he turned, sat down, and—listen to this—started to joyfully slide down the buttered rock, loudly shrieking: *'Ça, c'est la vie. Ça, c'est la vie.'* In English, that means, 'Now this is the life."

Winston laughs and so does Theodora. Even the stranger behind the tree is shaking with silent laughter. Wiping a tear from her eye, Theodora says, "Very funny story, but do you believe it?"

Still laughing, Winston replies, "It's a wonderful story, isn't it? For the end of a wonderful day."

"Wait," says Theodora quickly. "Are you still laughing? For a moment, I honestly thought I heard someone else laughing. How odd." She smiles. "Maybe it was our old friend the maple tree."

"Tomorrow, dearest Theodora, we will start a new life. We'll watch these beautiful sunsets from somewhere else. It's getting colder, you know. Our symphony of evening lights is over for now."

"What do you mean, tomorrow?" asks Theodora.

As if on cue, the stranger leaps from behind the tree, pistol in hand, and shoots and mortally wounds both of them from behind without any hesitation at all. He searches through the woman's dress until he finds the keys, takes the man's wallet from his back pocket, and goes triumphantly back down the forest path. Dusk turns quickly to darkness and night begins.

My beak fell open from shock and sadness. I decided to follow the murderer and, in my own way, to make him pay for his reprehensible behavior.

# God Bless America!
## A Theatrical Sketch

Set:       *A grocery store*
Players:   CUSTOMER, *a white man in his 50s*
           MOTHER, *a young, pretty woman (mute role)*
Plot:      *The customer, used to seeing his favorite salesperson pregnant, assumes that she has now had her baby. While he ignores the repeated dismissive waves of her hand, he gets into a harangue on "how valuable this birth is to our Nation in this time of stagnation of white birth rates, as opposed to the dreadful overpopulation of the Third World." His ironic, matter-of-factly given remarks on gluttony here and starvation there urge her to sneak away, leaving him a note which reads, "Sorry to disappoint you, but I had a stillbirth." (The way it is read must come as a shock to both the customer and the audience.)*

### CUSTOMER

Hello, hello! Good to see you again! Welcome back! How are you doing? It's so good to have you back in my all-time favorite shop. You look so well, so nice, so slender, to say the least. You're back to your normal shape, right? May I congratulate you? Childbirth is always a wonderful event, a cause for celebration. But ... Yes! You were gone for only a short while, if I remember correctly—and I do. Such a happy event demands a little more time, no? You look splendid, just a little bit pale still. And you can work again so soon after delivery. Wonderful, wonderful indeed! You must have found a good midwife and a possibly great wet nurse, no? Or do you have other reasons for being back so soon?

No, no, no… don't bother; it's your happiness that moves me. I can tell, you're happy. There is nothing in this world more satisfying than motherhood, is there? Yes, yes, nothing to a woman, any woman, I must add. Yet, you still do look a little pale after your delivery. Anything wrong? Don't... it's not my business to ask questions here. The main thing is that it came off and we have a new addition to the human race. And an American—bravo—who will work and pay taxes in the future to help finance pensions for our older generation. Ah, youth! Children are our own future, our best investment, as one of our presidents said, the only true annuity there is. Nobody would be entitled to receive pensions if it weren't for the younger generations who provide for them.

Another child of the earth, welcome, welcome. Let me guess ... boy or girl? Well, you rather look as if you gave birth to a boy, a sturdy, strapping young man—bravo!—one of those wolfish daredevils ready to conquer every woman's heart. Am I right? Just great! For now he'll enjoy your pampering *(he starts selecting goods)* and later he will plague the teachers at nursery school and then at school, and so on as we all did. Life always repeats itself so beautifully. *(He keeps piling canned food on the counter. She helps him, apparently knowing his choices. Each time she tries to interrupt, he declines her gestures.)* Yes, the usual. Thank you. What will the future bring? Will your little one be happy? Rich? Will he encounter better times than we do? Just imagining what's waiting for him, whatever might occur when we're long gone. We are doing fine today, aren't we? A few far-away wars that don't really bother us, they keep the military producers happy. What a world, living on destruction. Funny, huh?

But he ... your little one ... No, no, you don't have to tell me. I am so happy for you. I know of young mothers' enthusiasm, especially when it is the very first child and not the tenth or twelfth one as it is with our Mexican neighbor down the block where we have that poor, old-looking young mother with a dozen kids. A dozen, a dozen, and forever pregnant and no food—oh, yes... food stamps, yes, sure—they live off of us. No school, no education, not even learning English. All day long, hanging around in dirty clothes, a most terrible sight for the eyes of a true, white American, right? Right. And I ask you what do they contribute to our society? They do nothing, except extend the welfare roles and increase the pool of criminals. What a future! And we have to pay for their prison cells. Can't the government sort of restrict this kind of unwanted overproduction on their part? Don't we have pills … to …? Yes, yes, the pills only work on wealthy young white American women, not at all on them. Why? And abortion? Abortion is a sin, says the Church, says "Jesus," says the President. Can you imagine a president named Jesus? Would Jesus like to become an American president? I have my doubts. Would he win a war for us? Or, who would want him for a U.S. president, who? After all, the nails—as they say—are still ready *(coughs)*. I'm glad you didn't have an abortion. Of course, of course, I admit any woman's right to it. I'm pro-choice, and you know why? Mexicans and others do not know abortion, they don't. As you see, the wrong people go to the abortion clinics. It's true, isn't it? Me? A racist? Can't I just say what is on every white man's mind? No, not on everyone's mind.

Well, well, looking at you makes me happy. The sight of a healthy, young, well-to-do American mother, you're God-blessed, you are! *(Packing another item she hands him).* There, there, thank you, dear. Yes, this is my brand.

In a few weeks or a few months maybe, you will proudly introduce your little one to us, your best and faithful customers. I can't wait to see him. I'll share your happiness, may I? It's a gift from heaven, after all, a sign of grace. Remember this as you bring up your precious child! Yes, indeed, each child is a divine gift to the world, even those down there. We mortals have, of course, we have to give a helping hand to start the fire and keep it burning, so to speak, to bring the human and the divine seed to sparkle and to glow, and to grow. We catch the fire, but the fire comes from the Lord. Even the Pope has heard of it. How to do it, but he can't, he is not allowed to play with fire, ha-ha, not even he. Strangely enough, He condemns all abortion and birth control. Regardless of the cause!

For the Church, there cannot be enough children on earth to be baptized, right? Whether they starve or die of disease. Catholic priests are forbidden to use the divine fire, poor men. A priceless contradiction, isn't it? They applaud even the poorest born church mouse as long as it is born Catholic. The Pope blesses those who can't afford to have a child, to nourish a child. Is that a crime, or what is it? And the mothers in those hot, hot countries who give a damn about what the Bishop of Rome has to say keep producing babies. It might be a blessing for the rainforest that the coffins require so little wood.

For us here, it is truly a blessing to have a child. Isn't it awful to think that one day the white race might be extinct? What do you say? Maybe those Third World procreators do it knowingly to speed up the process? Apparently they don't care how many of their kids will starve to death as long as the survivors outnumber us. We are a dying race, aren't we? Well, I believe God speaks our language, doesn't he? He must. With his help, we are still alive and strong and win wars, occasionally. Oh yes, an American prayer recited with fervor can bring miracles to our recruitment problems. We don't pray enough nowadays. That's it. That's why we are experiencing such a lack of young blood, or is it too much fat in our food? What do you think? Maybe, it's because it isn't that much fun anymore, that catching of fire, no? Some marital partners—so I've heard—do pushups instead. *(coughs)* No wonder there aren't enough white babies being born.

We cultivated this vast continent over the years only to have a non-American population live on it—... The Indians? Oh yes, I forgot—while on the other side of the globe, what an overabundance, what an overproduction of humans. Of all people, it is the primitive ones, the poorest, who enjoy large families with pride. But you can't make something out of nothing. Their climate, yes, the climate helps to, to—you know what I mean.

Up here in the Northern Hemisphere, in these colder regions, you have to strongly wish to catch fire and have a result. Isn't it a totally crazy world? What we are longing for, they have too much, too many, that is… Down there, they don't have enough bread to feed their children while we spend billions on advertising for food that we produce too plentifully. Hardly anybody needs or wants to swallow it. A paradox, it is. All we can do is dabble in every new food created, nibble a little tipple of this and that. Food is a luxury item here compared to what the rest of the world has to bite into. We nibble on dainties and some look like pigs. Dreaming of more guzzling, more pigishness, more gluttony, more voraciousness, see how many words we have for the indulgence of our vices while others starve to death.

Artificial blood vessels are being created to rinse out the fat overdose in our livers, while our neighbors to the south don't have enough blood in their veins to fight the famine edema ... those poor, starving wretches. We know about this and remain perfectly unmoved. Do you understand that? I don't. Well, our government knows best what to do to keep us happy, why bother to waste a second thought on other people, right?

I can read your face. It tells me that you successfully contributed to save our Nation from menacing extinction. Very good! There will be grandchildren, sweet, curly-haired grandchildren. Congratulations, my dear. Congratulations to us! Ah, if only my sons had stayed home, we'd have more grandchildren and U.S. citizens. But no, they both had to leave for a "green" country, as if half of our forests weren't still green and robust, and as if our flowers weren't blooming anymore. Speaking of flowers, if I had known that you were back as a young mother, I'd have brought you some. Maybe next time? Besides, I've never met your husband, the happy, happy father of your child. It was rather empty here during your absence, I admit. This temporary worker, your substitute, truly couldn't replace you. He was an uncouth fellow, an awkward creature. I'm glad he's gone. Finally, I have my conversations again. It's so nice talking with you; this guy always cut me off. I could never say a word. Now that the child is born and you are blissful, it's very encouraging. Yes?

*(She has everything wrapped up for him and hands him the bill.)*

Oh, I'm sorry, I almost forgot to pay. Here! Thank you for all your help. How can you keep up with all these prices while taking care of your child at the same time? It is... yes? What?

*(She cries, nods, scribbles something for him, and leaves.)*

What is this? A note for me? Let's see. *(He reads it)*

"I am sorry to disappoint you, dear Mr. White, but I do not have a child. I had a miscarriage. The person who worked here was my dead child's father—at least he tried. Our nation better look for another woman to multiply its population. In view of the future, it might well be worthwhile to wait a bit. Maybe it is better for my baby not to be here. I wanted a child, but fate stepped in. Maybe it was for the best. I don't know. Good bye."

*(Mr. White becomes whiter than he already is and leaves the store in a daze, his thoughts filled with the loss to the poor rich nation. He doesn't see his neighbor from Mexico enter the store with nine of her twelve children, two in a stroller and one in a sling across her chest, to buy food with food stamps. Ah, America, the Land of Opportunity.)*

*End.*

# Made in Germany
## A Short Play

[How good it is to know that, besides mandatory material tests, there are also product presentations in the U.S., even if only internally, before the demonstrated products are put on the market. This short play portrays such a "presentation" of new products.]

PLAYERS:   ABE, *the president and CEO of Cheap Thrills & Co.*
SOL, *his sales manager and product designer*
LILA, *presentation girl in a swimsuit*

SCENE:   *Empty stage with a bathtub with a shower curtain, a sink, a beauty cabinet (standing or hanging), a rubber mat, a textile mat, plastic bath slippers, toothpaste and brush, toothpaste dispenser (plastic).*

PLOT:   *Sol presents the new product line to Abe. It is the bathroom equipment, the first models to be mass-produced by Cheap Thrills & Co. Sol surprises Abe by hiring sexy girl, Lila, to present the new products. The presentation turns out to be part of Sol's tactic to make higher profits by producing faulty products so that all of the items shown will soon break and must therefore be replaced. While Abe accepts this "trick," he falls in love with Lila, who playfully returns his advances. Praising junk "Made in the U.S.A." for profit's sake alone leads to the revelation that most, if not all, U.S. products are designed not to last—for faster consumption. When the presentation is over, the only item not "Made in the U.S.A." is the durable pair of slippers worn by Lila, which she has had for many years and which are labeled as being "Made in Germany."*

(A new, bright green bathtub is sitting on a raised platform and its shower curtain has been pulled closed. Two very comfortable upholstered chairs have been placed in front of the platform. Abe enters the company's presentation room wearing an elegant business suit and sits down to wait for Sol, who is obviously late. After a minute or so, he stands up, looking at his glistening watch, but then he sees a woman's silhouette behind the translucent shower curtain. She is obviously unclothed. He promptly sits back down and waits.)

(Sol enters at last, a fluttering silk scarf around his neck, apologizes three thousand times or so, plucking at his curled, pert handlebar mustache).

### SOL

*(Casually)* Shall we begin?

### ABE

*(Impatient, but only to see what's hiding behind the curtain)* Please, Sol! Show me what's new in our production line for fall.

### SOL

*(In a completely objective, unadorned tone)* Our design studio worked hard to present you with the first model in new trends for bathroom accessories, Sir! If this stuff is mass-produced, we'll rake in higher profits than ever.

### ABE

(Genuinely curious) How's that?

### SOL

*(Open about his production and sales strategy; they are behind soundproofed doors, after all)* We took some special care for this year's presentation to include some tricks to enhance sales.

ABE

*(Astonished)* Tricks?

SOL

Quality is out, you know. Short-lived items are in demand. But you know best what's hot and what sells.

ABE

What tricks?

SOL

To cut a long explanation short, sir, we designed little faults and errors into all things so they won't last.

ABE

*(Rather indignant)* Products of Cheap Thrills & Co. are famous for their durability.

SOL

*(Coolly)* And that's why we don't sell well. Change is the slogan of the new millennium, sir.

ABE

*(Somewhat mollified)* Go ahead and show me your scheme to double our sales.

SOL

*(Ice cold)* It's simple—by breaking things faster.

ABE

*(Defending his old ethos)* Isn't that against our standards?

SOL

*(With disarming cockiness)* When you're thinking profits, there's no place for higher values or… morality.

ABE

*(Defending his traditional thinking for the last time)*
I insist on durability in all our products, Sol.

## SOL

*(Undeterred)* I'll convince you with durable profits, Sir. I also have a surprise for you, a delight for the eyes.

*(Sol claps his hands. Lila pulls open the shower curtain, which rips apart; its rings break, too. She falls out of the bathtub, but keeps her TV smile while staggering around.)*
Here's... oops!

## ABE

*(Wants to assist, but Sol beats him to it)* Truly a small step for a model, but a giant leap for our product line. Welcome to Cheap Thrills & Company. What's your name, you darling little girl?

## LILA

*(With her unchanging TV smile)* My name is Lila, sir.

## ABE

*(Pulling on his tie, which seems to have suddenly become too tight for him)* And I am Abe to you—no sir, if you please.

## LILA

*(Begins her demonstration)* This is our latest model in contemporary bathtub design, Abe. The shower curtain is... was part of it, but it is replaceable, Abe. And it's so cheap.

## ABE

*(Mouth hanging open, almost enthusiastic)* Oh, Lila, I'll buy it; I'll get a new one, a transparent one.

## SOL

By cheap she means the new price, sir.

## ABE

*(Still can't believe it)* But that's indeed bad quality. It's junk.

### LILA

Modern life in modern bathrooms calls for swift and constant change, Abe. We produce what you like today, and if it breaks we'll replace it by tomorrow.

### ABE

*(Manages to stay professional, keeping one eye on Lila while ignoring the bathroom products completely)* And who, may I ask, pays for the damage?

### SOL

*(Jumps in for Lila, who wasn't drilled on this answer)* The customer does. We add tiny labels to everything that say, "Improper handling of this product may lead to its decay. No refunds will be given in such cases." Period. Now, let's demonstrate how quickly our customers will have to buy new items. Lila!

### LILA

*(Steps onto the mat and slides into Sol's arms)* Our all-synthetic fiber mats are made for fun, Abe.

### SOL

And they won't last long either. *(He tears it to pieces)*

### ABE

*(Torn out of his reverie of staring at Lila)* Hold it. That junk is our new quality?

### SOL

It's nothing, sir. Wait and see what else we'll sell to our customers over and over again. We'll outdo Wal-Mart and K-Mart, I promise.

### LILA

*(In a seductive, singsong voice)* No refunds, Abe.

### ABE

*(Desperate)* We've got a reputation.

## SOL

And declining sales. We can't leave our markets to cheaper Chinese production. We have to keep up with the Chinese. This is precisely the reason our new products are going to change the entire American market.

## LILA

*(Joins in the deadly sales babble)* Replacing and buying, Abe, buying and replacing is the future. Buy one, ruin it, and get another one. Buy two; get a third one free, Abe. Free market. *(She is able to wear a hole in the bath mat with ease, using her sturdy bath slippers)*

## ABE

*(Ensnared again)* Oh Lord, what a sweet voice you have, Lila.

## SOL

*(Sure of himself)* Numerous little built-in faults in these sensational new items—*(shouting)* Get back in the tub, Lila *(quieter)*—will turn our company's future rosy, sir. Anything made of plastic will break in time.

## ABE

I'm starting to like your idea. Wonderful. But tell me, what kind of warranty can we offer?

## LILA

Our everlasting smile and our ...

## SOL

*(Relieved that his strategy is working)* Take our new faucets, for example, the warranty for this set is one year. After a year and a day, it will fall apart. It will rust away rapidly. Lila!

## LILA

Our new faucets are so low to the sink that hand washing becomes almost impossible, Abe. Only if the tap is turned on

all the way will water gush out to reach dirty little hands, Abe
...

### SOL

Good thing we kept our contract with Waterworks. If we install these new low faucets in all of the 50,000 new homes to be built in our region this year, the water usage will be up at least 250 to 300 percent, sir.

### ABE

Great. I'll buy more Waterworks stock tomorrow.

### SOL

Because we install the faucets so low, they can hardly be cleaned at the base *(Lila demonstrates)*. Rust builds up quickly and will eat through the plastic rings as well. The result will be plenty of replacement sales.

### LILA

This is called thoughtfulness in planning, Abe.

### ABE

Your voice is so sweet, Lila. Why don't you talk for Sol? If your name had a "c" at the end, you'd be blooming in my backyard. I adore the smell of lilac.

### LILA

And if yours had a "c" or an "x" added, you'd be like a Swiss-made drooling machine, Abex.

### ABE

Oh, Lila, I'm drooling already.

### LILA

Wait, A-B-C. Save a little for after our presentation. *(She stretches her body lasciviously)*

## SOL

Our soap dishes are built in to make the water stay and melt the soap. I recommend buying stock in Soap Opera Unlimited as well, sir.

## ABE

*(To Lila)* Do you eat raw meat, sweet Lila?

## LILA

Abe. No, I'm a lusty veggie.

## SOL

Sir. The reason for selling our new products faster than last year lies in hidden secrets.

## ABE

I prefer unhidden secrets.

## LILA

Cracks, Abe, like these here in the bathtub are hardly visible, but they'll work.

## ABE

Enamel-covered plastic? We produce that now?

## SOL

Any clean-loving, dirt-hating *hausfrau* will face a losing battle. Yes, the metal frame is reduced to a mere 10 percent of what it used to be. The cracks will open, rust will build up, and then we'll send our free samples of "Enamel-Fill" to fix it. And that will even speed up the deterioration, sir.

## LILA

Our new "Fix-It-All" tubes have metal-eating chemicals added.

## ABE

Magnificent, girl! We'll sell much, much more. Are you... free?

### LILA

Tube and lube and nude in new bathtubs with hidden craquélé, Abe, what a pleasure to be free.

### ABE

Superb. What else? I'm going to melt.

### SOL

Why don't you show him our new toiletry products, Miss Lila?

### LILA

First, look at this, Abe. The new sink is constructed in such a way that the slightest excess weight placed on top of it will break its trimming off the wall, it will come right down. And no one can be blamed. Our stickers read: "Do not put items on the sink." Hah!

### ABE

You are ingenious. You're hired.

### SOL

Took the words right out of my mouth. And now let's see our little extras, sir.

### LILA

*(Demonstrates)* Here's our new toothbrush, see, Abe? It cannot be cleaned well and will rot away soon, or it will break *(demonstrates)*. The toothpaste dispenser has its tricks built in, too. I give it three months.

### SOL

Two months at the most.

### LILA

And here, the hinges on our new Happy Beauty Cabinet are made so thin that they'll split right away. Isn't it funny?

### ABE

Marvelous. We'll double our output—or triple it.

SOL

And we can reduce its ridiculous high price by half and we can still make a hefty profit, sir.

LILA

That's true also for the bathmat. It's plastic, not rubber and allows fungus to grow in those itsy-bitsy tiny rings underneath, which Sol created. Dirty bathwater will do its merciless work.

ABE

Fabulous. My wife hates athlete's foot.

SOL

Every two or three months, our dear customers will ask for and buy our new mats, sir. They're also slippery.

ABE

*(Applauding)* Splendid. What a great gesture. What about insurance?

SOL

Liability lays with the stupid customer, never with us, sir. Nobody ever reads the fine print.

LILA

I never read. I watch TV while I foam in my bathtub, Abe.

SOL

Also, we designed virtually invisible handling or installing fixtures, sir. They hold for a year and then... crash-bang. They'll come down. Our labels say: "No refunds if mishandled." All of our stupid customers mishandle our products.

ABE

Stupefying. We'll produce three times more than last year. Absolutely fantastic, Sol.

### LILA

If something will not come down, we'll come up with ideas to pop up what's left intact, Abe.

### ABE

Gorgeous girl. Nothing will last, wonderful. Our new president puts people first, and we put profit first. Ha.

### SOL

With constant praise on TV, we can turn the worst rubbish into the most wanted items. Anything goes in America.

### ABE

Splendid. Sol, you have my blessing to start on production. Lila, dear, whose are those pretty slippers?

### LILA

They're my own. The plastic ones that Sol gave me broke. *(Giggles)* They were our product, but I've been wearing these for over eight years.

### SOL

Are they ours, too?

### ABE

For heaven's sake, no junk.

### LILA

*(Taking one off)* Indeed, they're very solid, made from real leather, no rubber or plastic. The label reads—oh, no—"Made in Germany". I should have known.

(Shocked and rather unenthusiastic about this unexpected statement of quality, Abe leaves the presentation room, but slips Lila his card on the way out. Sol sees this and disappears with the pretty girl right away—no, not behind the torn shower curtain, but right into the bathtub, where they promptly undress. Only their legs are visible at the end of the tub, dancing in the air. On one foot is a leather slipper with the label "Made in Germany.")

***

Their happy ending didn't last for long. Barely three days after the in-house presentation, the treacherous Miss Lila, who had been working with the company as part of a government sting operation, introduced the company's product line herself on national television. She had recorded the presentation using a hidden camera and microphone, and the video flickered across most of the television screens in the country. The result? This highly celebrated line of junk products is now being produced by another company, which has not yet been busted.

(One of the author's playbills.)

 and

**CORDIALLY INVITE YOU TO ATTEND :**

**DEATH... and other earthly amusements**

AN EVENING OF DARKLY HILARIOUS
THEATRICAL SKETCHES

**by DirkHolger**

SUNDAY, APRIL 26TH, 8:00P.M.
1992

at Source Theatre Company
1835 14th Street, NW Washington, DC 20009
TICKETS $10,  PLEASE CALL 202-462-1073

sponsored by:

Stohlman Volkswagen/Subaru
8433 LEESBURG PIKE
TYSONS CORNER
VIENNA. VIRGINIA 22182

RECEPTION WITH PLAYWRIGHT
TO FOLLOW PERFORMANCE

# Sonia

"Where is Sonia?" asks my little one in the summer of 2001.

"She's gone for good, Robert, she'll never return."

"Where did she go?"

"In short, she is in a better place, in an eternal home which is far more peaceful than her home down here in Olney."

Little Robert looks at the empty wall near the sidewalk at the intersection of Morningwood Road and Georgia Avenue. "You know what, Papa? Maybe her ghost will be sitting there one day."

"Where?"

"Over there, on that low wall where she was always sitting. Maybe ..."

\*\*\*

Sonia is no more. She was the only visible homeless person in Olney, Maryland. For many years, she sat at the same street corner. She was almost a pretty sight, well-kempt, clean, with her bright straw hat to be seen from afar, were it not for the collection of plastic bags, her only belongings, surrounding her. She had no work, no goal, no schedule; no one was waiting for her. She never created unrest. Only one day did she "cause trouble" to herself, when she was thrown out of the local McDonald's. Witnesses said that she was not begging or bothering anybody. The little money she had, which paid for her plastic cup of coffee, she had brought with her. She fell asleep at her table. It was her bag collection that so disturbed the management, and the simple fact that she could sit for hours quietly in her corner. In a McDonald's, you must consume; you are not welcome to just sit down and warm up in winter or cool off on a hot summer day. McCharity does not exist.

We all carry our burdens, our bags, our bundle of guilt, with or without a label that says, "paid for." Sonia carried her bags out of necessity, she had no "shopping habits"—she was just homeless. Good souls like Joan and Louie (a pastor) who took her in on ice-cold nights wondered why she disappeared after a short while. It was her sign of a strong will for individuality and independence. She was a loner, not belonging to the unsightly group of bums and winos hanging out at routes 97 and 108, the busiest intersection in Olney. Keeping her distance from the other "forgotten ones" was her choice for solitude.

There she was, sitting quietly day in and day out. She slept upright with just her head down. No one has ever seen her lying down. She closed her mind to the outside world. A faint smile and a hushed "thank you" was all we got when we gave her a dollar. The not-so-well-to-do were the ones who supported her. If a rich lady passing by in her Jaguar were to cause an accident in front of her by doing her nails while driving, Sonia would not notice it. Only when we heard that she had passed away did we learn her full name and age through the obituary distributed by Joan and Louie.

Sonia, not a sight of misery and suffering, but an image of peacefulness, is gone and lives on in our memories. We miss her silent presence.

# I Hate MacDonald's
## A Satire

This story is not solely fiction. It could have happened anywhere in these All-Uniting States. To protect the identity of the participants in this 'field trip,' I use only their nicknames. I—the unimportant storyteller, with the healthy name of Cheers—hope that you, dear reader, have already eaten.

"Does anybody want a snack?" I ask over the school bus microphone. The answer is a raucous, howling "yes!" from the two school classes taking part in the field trip. To be more precise, I add, "I mean, do you want something fast, that is, junk food?" I have to cover my ears, so loud is the yelling of the "hungry pack." This, despite the fact that the children had their breakfast at school.

Mrs. Glut, our solidly built principal, takes the microphone out of my hand. "Mr. Cheers, you're only a chaperon. Let me speak! Classes! Children! You rowdy troublemakers! Listen up! Quiet! I'm the one who decides when and where we stop, got it?"

Neither I, nor Mrs. Solidario, our head chaperon, can contain the newly erupting noise, although we shout alternately into the microphone, "Pay attention!" "Be quiet!" "Listen!" and even "Shut up, all of you!" to no avail. Not the least discipline or respect is shown towards us, the adults. I had secretly hoped that Micah, my little one in the bus, who is joining in the shouting match, would have learned some manners in this elementary school, but far from it. He is as wild as the rest of his class and nudges those sitting next to him. The girl in front of him, Coco, picks her nose, totally unembarrassed, and the twins Alisha and Trisha, mimic her—a sorry sight.

Our bus driver, with the appropriate name of Miss Watchout, has an idea, and calls me to the front. While she continues to drive the bus safely and soundly, I hold the microphone to her mouth. She is the only black person among the adults and all of the school children like and respect her. She speaks very convincingly: "You little brats! You aren't going to get one bite unless you shut your big mouths." Her not-so-subtle admonition works wonders. A sudden hush falls over the students, much to the astonishment of Mrs. Glut, our uncheerful principal, who has pursed her lips indignantly. Miss Watchout continues:

"Which one of you howling monkeys can count to a thousand? 'Cause I'm telling you, this bus isn't stopping till you've counted to one thousand!"

The busload of 7 to 8 and 9 to 11 year old youngsters takes the bait and a noisy, confusing, bewildering counting starts. After only a few seconds our comic, Buddy, has arrived at "133, 134, 135" while the well-behaved girls in the front rows are correctly counting "12, 13, 14, 15…"

I whisper into our leader's ear, wondering whether we could drive straight through to our destination, the "Merryland Farm," instead of interrupting the trip. She shoots a look at me as if I came from the moon.

"Mr. Cheers, the snack was your bright idea, not mine. We'll stop when the girls from my class have counted to one thousand as Miss Watchout instructed. It's well over an hour to the farm and there isn't any food out there but fruit."

The way she pronounces the word expresses her dislike of fruit quite eloquently. I keep silent; I have no chance against the official voice. As one of the volunteers, I have zero authority.

Eric, who, at eleven, is the oldest member of the two classes, beckons me to his seat. After I arrive at his row after quite some shuffling, the twins, Alisha and Trisha, grin at me as if I knew the reason for their obvious happiness. What does Eric want? He asks me very quietly, with a blushing, "Mr. Cheers? Can't we stop somewhere—anywhere—please? I have to pee."

What should I do? "I'm sorry, Eric, you must squeeze your legs together until Mrs. Glut orders a stop." He does squeeze his legs together and whimpers. Meanwhile, my little Micah next to him, has reached "98, 99, Papa, 100!" while others are already past 300. It feels good to see that some of the children are doing their counting in a civil manner, in a low voice, but they are the exception among the screaming horde.

From the very last row in the bus, a loud belch can be heard over the noise. It comes, oddly enough, from Samantha, a petite, almost emaciated girl, who seems far too small to be making such a large sound. Her digestive problems are really no surprise; it is an open secret that she suffers from bulimia, gorging herself and then sneaking to the bathroom to throw it all up. The cycle of gluttony and self-hatred is painful to watch, and the effects are not just psychological. On the rare occasions when she smiles, you can already see the damage to her teeth caused by overexposure to stomach acid. Like Mrs. Glut, she is a casualty of modern American eating habits. She is a casualty of pop culture as well. The near-unattainable ideal of thinness is a dangerous combination with the fast food ads that tout their food as a quick fix and easy route to happiness ("We love to see you smile"). So, along with countless other American girls, she continues the cycle of binging and purging, of eating and self-hate. She stares quietly at the tops of her shoes, her face almost hidden by her long hair. Is she a calming influence? I almost wish she were as agitated as her classmates.

"Hey, Samantha's belching again—and man, her breath stinks." With these indelicate words, Ken, everyone's favorite loudmouth, interrupts his counting and pinches his nose theatrically.

Sudden, wild gesturing by the students in the window seats points out a sign along the road. It is the accursed yellow 'M' sign, the trademark of bad mass eating habits, the international symbol for junk food. My question in the beginning for a snack was meant to be ironic and a test, which went completely wrong.

How could I have been so blind? Thanks to the daily bombardment in all the media of persuasive commercials has led the American youth astray and they have fallen prey to the total seduction of fast food. It bothers nobody to know that the United States spends more money on marketing the overproduction of its food than for actually producing it. How perverse is that? As eating habits become more generic, the American society is becoming more and more uniform, gaining a new identity by losing its once-prized individuality in a radical way.

My thoughts about this saddening aspect of American society and the boisterous counting of the kids are both cut short by a loud, joyful scream of "Macdonald's!!" Of all bad things, it is junk food that makes them happy. I begin to have second thoughts about having volunteered for this field trip, knowing that all of the students are for hamburgers and I am the only one against that meat mush. I confess that I have a profound aversion for this indefinable, tasteless, squashy stuff. Yes, I hate it.

Here are some of the reasons why I hate junk food. As I visit the United States so often, I see a direct relationship to the eating habits of the average American, an incomprehensible lust for devouring red meat (more than any other food, it seems) and their daily behavior and illnesses.

Obesity is the most visible, starting at an alarming rate among the young. Aggressiveness is another and not only to be witnessed in rude driving ("road rage" is the new term). I even blame the country's high criminality on both the excessive eating of flesh, and, you must believe this, on the excruciating methods of producing the red meat. On top of this comes the strange belief of the masses that "what my neighbor eats, (buys, plays with, watches, reads, does) must be good for me, too." This is clearly more a mania than a mere illusion, and, of course, not only in the United States. I also refuse to believe that "ketchup" has the ability to render a hamburger tasty. Oh, how my taste buds recoil at the very thought of this combination of meat and tomato sauce. I am also glad to say that I know of quite a few Americans who enjoy good food and delicate eating and do not set foot into any of the fast food chains, ever.

From another row in the bus, a deep snoring can be heard over the noise. It comes, small wonder, from "Chief," who, like Mrs. Glut, suffers from "eating disorders," as gluttony is being labeled in these progressive days. He eats far too much and far too often and that makes anybody tired, child or adult. He is in the arms of Morpheus (the god of sleep and dreams) in the middle of the school bus chaos. Chief is an American Indian, a pale redskin, who lacks pride in his heritage. His only difference from the rest of the class is his oversized body, a shame for a Sioux Indian. There he sits and sleeps and puts on even more fat.

"Hey, Chief's farting in his sleep." Ken again, supplying his perpetual stream of color commentary.

I can hardly believe my own ears as Miss Watchout grumbles, "I hate Macdonald's." Well, there, I am not alone! Mrs. Glut, of course, cannot allow such blunt individual expression of free speech. She brings the loudness of the lively kids to a temporary halt with a whistle and turns to the bus driver to reprimand her. "Kindly keep your preferences and dislikes to yourself, Miss Watchout. By the way ..." she licks her plump lips, "we will pass by two or three more M signs. I know this route very well!" (Unfortunately, she does.)

"How can anybody hate Macdonald's?" Mrs. Solidario asks the bus driver in a deep voice with a slight Hispanic accent. "Why, Miss Watchout? My kids, like Alida here on the bus, eat there often and we like it."

"Oh yes, and I know why," Miss Watchout responds almost cheerfully. "You catch more flies with honey than with vinegar."

Mrs. Solidario's eyes signal a question mark, as she obviously does not understand this expression, and she looks at me. I just shrug my shoulders.

Pushing me aside (I am "Euro-trash" in her eyes), Mrs. Glut approaches the bus driver again to remind her of this.

"Later, Miss Watchout, later, when we have stopped at Macdonald's and not a second before, you may feel free to explain poor Mrs. Solidario your very weird aversion for what constitutes our national eating culture. And you Mr. Cheers? What are you grinning about, huh?" She turns back to the bus driver. "You just concentrate on safe driving and absolutely nothing else. I am in charge of keeping the kids in good spirits." How I would love to explain my own reasons for my dislike of the mass food as well, but I keep silent, for the moment.

"Why do you want to spoil the students' appetite?" Mrs. Glut mutters as if she could read my thoughts. "Perhaps it's because you cook differently in your own country. Hmm?" She says this while giggling.

Actually, I had a good answer to her insinuating question. Still, I prefer to keep it to myself and instead, flash her a big smile, which she enjoys not at all.

She turns away and asks over the microphone, "Anyone counted to one thousand yet?"

Immediately, the students yell: "I did," or "We counted to two thousand," "I'm already at five million, stop the bus," then this: "I'm hungry." That perks up Samantha right away. Another, softer voice can be heard, "I have to go to the bathroom." I feel sorry for Eric.

"You settle down, you noisemakers," is all that our large leading lady has to offer and she asks Miss Watchout, "Did you hear? Your fabulous counting game is over. As soon as you see the next M sign, get off the road. We're stopping there," she says without the barest indication of a please.

Less than a mile farther down, the sign can be seen high above the trees and roofs as the all-dominating advertisement and alluring symbol for fast junk food. ("I'm not in Europe anymore.")

The very sight of it upsets my stomach. But this time, at least it stands at the entrance to a mall with probably several other eateries and thus a greater choice of food. ("Rejoice, you ruins of my hurt tummy!") Those other restaurants usually serve their own stereotype menus, but they vary from one location to the next. They also offer real, freshly squeezed juices, and not the sugar-syrup-water-soda. I dare to ask Mrs. Glut if the bus driver and I could lunch at one of these other places, but her answer comes like a hissing, "Are you nuts? You stay with the kids. Period!"

Before we turn off, I get to hear even more of the typical American dependence on advertising—from the kids. Mack, an otherwise intelligent boy, says to Roxy, a black girl sitting next to him, "I could give up anything else—just not my hamburgers."

"Do you know how much good stuff there is in a Big Mac?" she asks.

Mack laughs. "More good stuff than there is in me! But they said on TV last night 'strength and joy and happiness/and lots of protein in excess' is in every Big Mac."

She sings, "We love to see you smile."

Mack nods, "And it's just as good all over the world."

"And there's love in it! They make it with lots of love."

I respond only inside my head. Yes, there's love in there all right. Love for sweetened fat. Should I admit it openly? The omnipresence, no, not of God's Word, but of uniform meat-eating seduction in the media, it sickens my soul.

I manage to sneak up close enough to our bus driver that I can whisper a question in her ear. "Why do you hate Macdonald's?"

Here is her astounding answer: "Ya'know, Mr. Cheers, the masses are just as dumb all over the world. If not, Macdonald's helps make up the difference. Believe me, eating this crap makes you stupid. It's a deliberate enticement to bad eating, to bad taste, an unscrupulous strategy by the manufacturer."

She sighs, and I add my sigh to hers. "That's how it is. I see it, too. And the whole thing has gone global."

Screeching, the bus stops in the fast food chain's parking lot. (Old, unchecked brakes, an accident waiting to happen, I'll have to report it.) I count (with unease) around seven, then eight, M signs, with just as many on the other side of the building. Promotion is absolutely everything here.

Mrs. Solidario and Mrs. Glut have their hands full trying to keep the shoving, shouting, and young horde streaming out of the bus in some sort of order. It is the American version: no orderly lines, no goosesteps, just an excited, pushing, laughing school class, or two, led on by the large M, heading for the trough. I really do think of pig fodder—pardon me! Mrs. Glut secretly sticks a few cookies into her great, fleshy mouth, earning her nickname all over again.

Surprisingly enough, Mrs. Solidario shares our desire; if we can't go to a real restaurant, then at least we should eat somewhat apart from the two loud school classes. In a fit of generosity, our large leader accedes to our request. Mr. Darkbeer, our third chaperon, joins us once the gigantic order of more than 40 burgers and hot dogs has been placed. We help to distribute the plastic flatware and are astounded at how quickly the order is filled—truly a fast restaurant. To the horror of the employees, we adults order only salads for three of us. Mrs. Solidario orders a hot dog. (Should we perhaps ask her if she knows the etymological connection between the long, red thing on her plate and the thing that shows a dog to be "hot," or in heat? Probably not.) Miss Watchout, Mr. Darkbeer, and I exchange significant looks.

We have hardly sat down away from the hubbub on plastic chairs at a plastic table with our plastic plates and our "salads" in plastic boxes, each of us with a cup of so-called coffee (in America, it seems as though one cup of European coffee is diluted to about 10 or 12—thin, brown, watery stuff) in garish plastic cups, with real and synthetic sugar, when a commotion starts at a table with the boys. Ken has (supposedly) put too much ketchup (red-colored stuff used as a taste-killing, all-purpose sauce) on Mack's hamburger and my Micah (supposedly) took away his plastic cup in retaliation and dumped a corresponding amount of salt and pepper packets onto Ken's burger. Well, that doesn't make it any more appetizing.

Mrs. Solidario rushes over to pacify the three fighting ruffians—and succeeds. As a "thank you" they treat her to a few potent expressions from their elementary school vocabulary that take her breath away.

"Without ketchup, even a dummy like you can't have sex." (Nine years old) "That's no reason to mess up my burger, you stupid son of a b----." "You shut both your filthy mouths, salt and pepper are good for your pimples in your face and on your brains, you complete idiots." "You're a racist, Mack. You don't like blacks, just like your old man. Everybody knows that's why they put him in jail, you stinking dirtball." "And you? You stink like a skunk. Doncha have a shower at home?" "You're rotten and crazy ..." "Shut the f--- up!"

There were other such friendly remarks. The girls at the next table look at them appraisingly and with some disgust.

America and its racial problems, it is a peaceful side-by-side rather than a tolerant, understanding cooperation, an eternal conflict. To make good for the racial tensions in this society, the entire nation, all races, from Alaska to Florida, eat the same meals in the same junk food joints, day in and day out. That's "poetic justice."

At a table behind us, an older couple sits down noisily, the plastic chairs, seeming to bend under their weight, squeak. Miss Watchout whispers into my ear, "They look like they've gorged themselves enough already. I bet they each swallow more than one burger." The overweight man gets up with difficulty, waddles over to the counter, places his order and returns as if swaying were the only way he can move forward to meet his better (fatter) half.     Thank heaven; Mr. Darkbeer distracts our attention from this sorry sight with his comments.

"In my eyes, d'you want to hear this, anything being served here is trash, plain trash, not food at all. You could use this McRubbish to feed animals or fertilize the back yard, but to me these 'meals' are an insult. They offer neither nutrition nor flavor, just plain junk. They've got the right name."

"Well, well," is all Mrs. Solidario says. By now Miss Watchout is ready to unload her very own, not-so-friendly thoughts about fast food.

"Someone on channel 69 said recently that it takes a genius to create a standardized hamburger. Do you know what?" I listen with pleasure.

"It is a stroke of genius for the profiteers alone. For those poor souls in the slaughterhouses and the meatpacking houses who produce the basics at minimum wages, it's an entirely different picture. It is the most horrific job imaginable. As if shoving any edible or digestible parts of a cow through the grinder were brilliant. The idea itself is not so bad. My grandparents used to grind up leftovers from our meals, but then we knew exactly what was in it. Then they made nicely spiced dumplings from it and fried them. But here? To put the thin, flat, uniform blobs of meat between two mushy, sweetened halves of a bun, my Lord, what a tasteless combination. Grilled caterpillars taste better ... It's the sweetening of everything that gets the kids addicted, that's the main reason why they love this worthless stuff so much... yuck. I started trying to lose weight about six months ago, and this crap is the first thing I cut out. And you know what? I really don't miss it at all."

"Did you know?" adds Mr. Darkbeer, "that officially only 80 percent of the burgers have to be meat?"

"Is that true or did you make it up?" Mrs. Solidario wants to know.

Miss Watchout has the answer. "I read that too, somewhere in the paper maybe. And I have no desire to find out what the other 20 percent consists of, or I'll run to the bathroom."

"It is common knowledge," I dare to elaborate, "that the 'beeeef' ..." (I pronounce a word in such way that it sounds despicable) "...is in most cases not the pictured bull or steer that they show, but a cow. Anything with some fat on that cow, be it the ears, the udder, the tail, the legs, the snout, the belly, everything gets ground up in huge machines, big as buildings, crushed, squeezed, squashed, mashed, mushed, and mixed until that pink, white-red, gooey paste forms, in which meat is no longer perceptible as meat. Even toothless people can easily swallow it. Then salt and sugar and a whole lot of antibiotics are added to give the mush some sort of flavor and on top of that, when the stuff is formed into those flat, round pieces and broiled, the red, uniform tomato-sauce-slush, made from virtually unknown ingredients, gets squeezed out on top of it and the whole unsightly something gets garnished with unappetizing pickles, served on a plastic dish, and then ... devoured. God-awful!"

"It makes me sick to the stomach to watch the slurpers over there gulping it down. My son Micah, too, has long given up using his knife and fork. The fist shoves the fat Big Mac into the jaws, opened as wide as the piece of junk is big. And? That's one more sign, a dreadful one, of our relapse back into the Stone Age." No one laughs.

"To add insult to the senses, shrill pop music is poured out of hidden loudspeakers, and ... yes?"

Mrs. Solidario derails my train of thought. "Enough. Shouldn't we be helping Mrs. Glut by now?"

Mr. Darkbeer, who was hiding his talents and keeping suspiciously silent at the start of our field trip, explains.

"Dear Mrs. Solidarnosz, pardon me, Mrs. Solidario, don't you worry. We have hired girls from the upper grades as volunteers to keep the two classes somewhat under control. Look over there, it has almost calmed down except for the sounds of smacking, grunting and slurping and the usual merry teasing." He turns to me.

"Well, Mister, your name amuses me, dear Mr. Cheers. I'd like to hear more about what you have to say about this fabulous fast food feeding frenzy. So go ahead!"

I almost raise my eyebrows, but manage to stay composed. "Who would not prefer to eat from genuine porcelain?" I answer. "Like in a normal restaurant, with cloth napkins and with silverware for forks and knives and—" (Krrrrk! my plastic fork breaks with a little pressure on the cold, hard cucumber.)

"Excuse me, please?" I ask and get up to fetch another set of plastics when I overhear the following (and I'm not making this up) as I pass a table with a family of four, three of them "overeaters anonymous."

"Do you know, Vaughn, why some people, even politicians in high positions in Europe, call our new president a village idiot? Do you?" (Mr. Darkbeer later gave an answer to the embarrassing question: "Because you can't criticize a dimwit!")

On the way back to our table I happen to catch yet another question, albeit only half of it.

"Is it true that Gore lost the election because of the heavy (inaudible) ... influence and the Bush campaign won with the finances from (inaudible again) ... by the ..."

Sitting down without further contemplating the still burning questions about the obvious voter fraud in Florida's election, I tell Mr. Darkbeer my humble opinion about this place where we are stuck today due to school coupons.

"Like you, I can't stand to eat with plastic from plastic…" ("Is there life after plastic? I doubt it…")

"…But the worst of all is the throw-away mentality of these fast food chains and their customers. Everything is disposable. The daily, tremendous garbage heaps…"—I stretch this word as long as the Rocky Mountains are wide—"…of plastic trash created with intention and full purpose by Macdonald's should give the fast food eaters a second thought about ... what ...?"

At this moment, Molly, one of the older helpers, comes rushing to our table and reminds us, "Most of the forty burgers are eaten. What about you? Why are you still at your salad? Mrs. Glut says it's really important that we all leave at the same time, all of us." And she's off.

We eat a bit faster at what is called a "salad," but have to listen to some very loud newcomers at a table next to ours. A mother with her son of excessive weight, who howls at her, "I'm still hungry. Go on, Mom, order me two more, noooooow!"

"What? Are you out of your mind? You just ate four double burgers in the other mall and now you want even more? I just came here for a drink. Look in a mirror! I've got a piglet for a son, a disgrace to our family."

That does it. The big little one bangs his fist down so hard on the plastic table he makes it clatter and screams even louder, "You're not a mother. You're starving me."

She calmly responds, "Listen, pig boy. Even if you didn't cram yourself full for three weeks or eat a morsel at all, you might lose a few pounds, but starve? You? Never. Sorry." Flailing his short arms, the fat boy marches resolutely to the counter to still his hunger without mother, and to not starve himself to death. Disgusted, we all turn our heads away from this tragic family comedy.

From the very next table—we are boxed in as the only salad eaters among flesh eaters—we can bear witness to a new conversation. Two carpenters probably, judging from their habits and dress, are evidently unhappy with their burgers, which they push half-eaten to the middle of the table. Now they too are doing their share of political talk.

"I'm not one of those who voted for the Texan, no, not me," one of the carpenters said.

"Yeah, what's going on in our country?" his partner responded. "Is he really as dopey as everyone says? Can anybody ever wipe that smirk off his face?"

The question was answered with a question. "Do you think he's going to lick the boots of his supporters like that tax-evader with the Israeli passport who got pardoned by Clinton? Pardoned, against all logic and reason! What?"

The other guy lowers his voice, but we still catch his warning. "Watch out! You can think about it, but you can't bring it up in public. Never! See, how far we've come with our so-called freedom of speech? You can't talk. You get crucified for it. Isn't it a shame?"

"It sure is, but I won't shut up, I always speak my mind, always."

"You better not." Both swallow their frustrations along with their cold burgers and leave in a rush.

"They're right, unfortunately, they are," Mr. Darkbeer says, revealing his political thinking.

"You can't express your own mind or—try to bring up a well-known fact—small wonder. Those at the top have the say and *pecunia non olet* [money does not stink]. And who has it? You tell me." He starts to sing.

"'Money makes the world go round, the world go round.' The truth is, there is really no difference between pigeons and politicians—when they are down they eat out of your hand and when they are up they crap on you, right? Right. Add the fix of the Florida election and you get the picture."

Miss Watchout takes her turn. "Maybe this oil cowboy is under the influence of the moralizers. Just listen to their old commandments, condemning anyone who is not on their side with hatred and contempt. I'd prefer even Clinton with his false pardons, who mistook the Oval Office for an amusement park. Hi, Molly!"

Again, Molly runs over urging us to rush. "It's hard to believe, but all of the hamburgers and the ton of fries have been polished off. In a few moments the brawl will start up again. Except Samantha and Chief have ordered a second serving and Eric is still in the bathroom. Please hurry!"

Hardly has she spoken these words when the verbal battles begin. "It's time." With these words, Miss Watchout gets up and leaves her half-eaten salad in the plastic bowl. "It's no loss of calories or anything if I don't finish it. I'll wait at the bus for you, okay?"

"Fine with me," says Mrs. Solidario, but she calmly continues to eat her "meal."

Nor does Mr. Darkbeer rush or move. He now comments (to my growing pleasure).

"With oil and vinegar it might be possible to enjoy these shredded greens, but not with the dressing they offer in those gaudy plastic tubes, no, not for me. I can do without. I'll be ready to leave soon."

He sips his coffee. I sip mine. We are in no rush and watch with some amusement as Mrs. Glut tries to get the two classes to line up. She recognizes how pointless it is and shoos the kids away and out of the plastic restaurant. As she passes Samantha, she manages to grab a handful of her fries and pushes it unseen down her throat. She calls this a "little nibble," as is all her eating. Near the door, a shouting match starts. Alisha and Trisha, our twins, return and address us instead of their teacher.

"Everybody got a plastic toy with their meal, but we didn't. The two of us got nothing. The others did," they bawl. "We're the only ones who didn't get a toy."

This must be settled at once. The plastic toys are part of a strategy to seduce the kids to bad, fast eating and we all share the same desire for our poor children to fall for this seduction, don't we?

I ask the friendly-faced man behind the counter wearing a name tag "Timi Oladipupo, Manager" why the girls did not get their plastic paraphernalia. With super-white teeth in his super-black face he smiles at me. "Sorry, but we had such a run on them today, they're all gone with the meals. I'll order new ones. Here's a coupon that entitles them to a free meal on their next visit here and…" He scribbles something on it. "I wrote here that they should each receive a double set of 'crazy bones,' I guarantee it. May I go do my other job now?"

"You may, and thank you very much."

He calls after us, "Please come back any time!" (With so much friendliness, one might feel inclined to return.)

Then we are all out of the door. Even Samantha has finished her clandestine trip to the restroom and scuttles out behind the rest of the students. Nina, the other helper, tells the principal with shiny eyes, "Your class is so well-behaved. I'd be glad to be a volunteer again next time." (She must be hard of hearing, or have poor eyesight.) "But, Mrs. Glut, I just ate and I feel hungry again."

"Off to the bus!" is Mrs. Glut's only response.

Mr. Darkbeer holds the girl back, "I am sure they add appetite stimulants to their food, otherwise you wouldn't be hungry so soon after a hamburger. Nina, just wait till we reach the farm where you can eat better food, like fresh fruit."

"Fruit? Ugh!" She makes a face and walks away. ("An apple a day keeps the doctor away." This wonderful epigram seems to have lost its meaning these days.)

Now I get my lecture from Mr. Darkbeer. "Have you read that book by Eric Schlosser called, *Fast Food Nation*? It's all about his research on the production of hamburgers—and it's honest to the point that the American Meat Industry Association protested against it. You—everyone—must read this book. Then we wouldn't have so many people getting addicted to Macdonald's and other junk food."

He has piqued my curiosity. "Can I find the book in our local library? What else is in it?"

"Mr. Cheers, you'll be on a waiting list there. You may as well buy it and, after you have read it, you'll want to lend it to family and friends as I did. I am convinced that most of its readers will stop eating hamburgers from any fast food chain. What I didn't know before is the fact that our government can recall any defunct toaster, but not contaminated meat. Isn't that alarming and shocking? Isn't that terrible? Eric Schlosser saw with his own eyes the deplorable working conditions in the slaughterhouses, how the butchers stand knee-deep in blood, how a stench of manure fills the air. Also, he found out that there are so many antibiotics in the meat one can get sick from the sheer knowledge of it. Until 1997, did you know it was lawful, just listen, to feed the plant eating cattle ground-up meat from other cows, from sheep, pigs, horses and even from dogs and cats that passed away in animal shelters—all that mixed with the regular grain food to get the cows fat faster. Isn't that disgusting?"

Miss Watchout answers for me. "It makes me want to throw up. Why would anyone feed ...?"

"Because," he continues, "the use of carcasses came cheaper than producing grain and hay, that's why. From 1997 on, it is still lawful—thanks to the government's dependence on the meat industry and the fast food lobbies—to add dead cows, pigs, horses, bone marrow, chicken, and even the manure of chickens to the feeding trough, plus all those unknown additives. Anybody who does not feel a stomachache should keep going to the fast feeders and enjoy their terrible stuff if they can."

Mrs. Solidario is appalled. "If that is true, and I will read it, I shall persuade my kids not to go to Macdonald's anymore, honestly. This is horrible."

"Or to any other burger chains either," Mr. Darkbeer adds. "We should all visit the slaughterhouses once, not as inspectors, but as hungry hamburger eaters, to see what Eric Schlosser experienced: the horrific stench when they kill the cows and remove the guts—up to 300 within one hour. That makes up to 800,000 pounds of raw, mashed burger paste in one day in any one of the many meatpacking facilities. In one day! Any single burger may contain meat and other material from up to 100 different cows, including, of course, sick ones, and more than just traces of feces. If that doesn't spoil your appetite ..."

I interrupt. "What you report is much more hideous than I ever thought. I'm horrified."

"That's not all," Mr. Darkbeer carries on. "The working conditions of the meatpackers, about 100 percent immigrants, are such that their job is being labeled the 'most dangerous' in all American industries. About one third of them are injured every day. Their blood gets splashed on what you eat when you eat what they produce. Just don't tell your children; they might well change their minds and stop eating and munching that meaty mess and look elsewhere for plastic toys. It would be disastrous to the meat industry if the population learned that, and I quote from Eric Schlosser's book, 'on any given day some 200,000 Americans get infected by food poisoning, 900 of them end up in a hospital and on average 14 of these die—every day.' You want to be one of them? Then keep 'enjoying' their junk food!"

We look at him, totally dumbfounded.

"I see," says Miss Watchout, "that's the reason these fast food joints broil the burgers through and through, until you could use them as insoles—the heat might kill off some of the many pathogens in it. May I make a suggestion?" (Her suggestion, of course, was denied by our parent-teacher association. It received "support" from the meat chains.)

"Lets have a special meeting of all of our school parents to educate them about the danger of infection when consuming meat products at Macdonald's, or other chains, and to ask any and all school classes to refrain from eating at those places when going on field-trips. We might take a first step to guard our own health and our children's."

All of us, including Mrs. Solidario, who turned quite pale during the arguments, agree to do 'something.'

We are just about to board the bus when we hear a scream of joy coming from the M building. We see the employees dancing and jumping for joy and embracing each other. One of the pretty black girls opens the door and calls to us, brimming with excitement, "We made it! He's coming to visit us. Just us. Yeah!" As the last one in line, I ask, "Who's coming, and what is he coming for?"

Almost ecstatic, she replies, "Our restaurant was selected for the visit of the most famous French chef of our time. He's in the U.S., just arriving, close to us and he picked our place out of thousands of others at random. Isn't it exciting?" She acts as if she is out of her mind with joy.

"What would be exciting about that?" This is actually not what I'd like to know but I ask it for all the curious faces behind me. None of the kids is willing to board the bus now, but Mrs. Glut commands them in.

"He ... the ... Mister.. I forgot his name," the girl calls back. "He has never in his life eaten a hamburger and will taste his first one here, at our restaurant. He'll get paid for it; it's the start of a new ad campaign. Isn't that great? Live on TV! Three TV stations are rushing to us. We'll get a hefty bonus today. The chef will be here in less than three hours, will you come back, please? Kids are good for background extras." To my dismay, Mrs. Glut has already made up her mind.

"Of course, we'll be here. If Monsieur Droldegout (I think that means Mr. Oddtaste in English) wants to have his first taste of Macdonald's, then we will bear witness with pleasure," she says emphatically. "How wonderful! How extraordinary!"

"Who's that? Mister ...?" Mrs. Solidario shyly asks. As if our principal had waited for the question, she explains.

"This is sensational! He's the world's best chef. I've seen him on so many kitchen shows on public TV, he gets countless offers to demonstrate his exquisiteness. So far he has regarded any typical American cuisine as undeserving of his comment. He always shows his disdain for our national food. Now, this will become a roaring promotion for Macdonald's. The best they could hope to get. They can count themselves lucky— congratulations, congratulations." She, too, appears ecstatic.

After giving our (her) word to return and serve as extras, we finally get on the bus, instruct Miss Watchout to change the return route and begin our second half of the drive to the Merryland Farm. A large, luscious orchard welcomes us there. The two classes get separated, the first one with the younger kids takes a hay ride, while the second class invades the various stables to smell genuine manure of cows, horses, sheep, pigs, chicken and to watch a huge flock of geese being fed fresh corn. Later in the market hall, a dozen of apple-varieties are being explained with the clear remark that all fruits grown here are free of pesticides and insecticides.

"Our harvest is free of any artificial additives," one sign reads. A mere handful of students chooses to take the chance and bite into a fresh, untreated, free apple. Fresh fruit seems to be an unknown food source to this youth. Had the invitation been for sweets, there would have been a stampede. Then we wander through the amazingly complicated hay maze, bumping into each other at unexpected corners, a late summer's day fun.

For us, the adults, this all-too-short stay at the farm is sheer relaxation. The breeze of fresh, unpolluted air, the fragrances of fruits, vegetables and fruit juices (we each take a gallon of apple cider home) feels so good. We taste about everything the farmer offers. The noise of the children is swallowed by the expanses of the vast, open fields. Only the thought that we have to return to the fast food joint by order of the principal dampens our enthusiasm. As we still savor the beauty of the rich, natural surroundings, the stillness and summery mood of leisure is slowly altered by the approaching return of the noisy classes. I collect my thoughts about what I like and dislike about this country and come to the conclusion that, in order to like the U.S. even more, I wish I didn't hate quite a few of the disturbing 'things' which come to mind. I make up a quick checklist about what I hate:

I hate:

- **Hamburgers**, of course, and not only those from Macdonald's. I terribly dislike any of the fast food chains for one reason: the elimination of individual taste.
- **Fast-chicken places** too. No eater wants to know—but, alas, I do—how the poor little creatures are mistreated before they land as appetizing-looking, small, "golden-brown" refigured portions, on your plastic plate.
- **The constant stream of music and blaring advertisements** wherever you go. See Charlie Chaplin in *A King in New* York!

- **Canned laughter,** where idiotic laughing groups get paid to laugh at TV scenes in which I find not the faintest trace of humor.
- **Moralizers in the media:** If Jesus saw or heard their money hustling in his name, he would surely swing his belt again.
- **Government censorship, anywhere.** And I hate the stupidity of the military, but what do you expect of people who act on orders?
- **"Lawn mania,"** Especially do I hate the totally green, but totally dead, lawns that are treated with weed killers and other toxic herbicides, replacing meadows until any and all insects and bees and bumblebees and butterflies ("flutter-bys," as little Robert calls them) are dying out.
- **Deforestation in the name of progress.** It is getting out of control—for each new house, at least 10 to 20 trees must be cut down.
- **Plastic:** Is there anything left in this world that's not made of it? Even the noses of the seducers from Hollywood are made of plastic. **Gun maniacs.** After shooting rampages in schools, fanatics declare, "it's not the gun that kills, but the finger that pulls the trigger." **Double standards** of those who prey on my soul—and the growing violence on TV—despite all empty promises, it is becoming more widespread since it sells well and is good for ratings.
- **Sports idols**, who rake in millions, but can't spell their last names.
- **I-don't-care attitudes and air-and-water polluters.**
- **State-sponsored terrorism, racism, and all sort of prejudices.**

The hate list seems endless, but so is my list of what I love here. You will find them in my short stories and, just for good measure, dear reader, I will include a list here of the things that I love.

I love:

- **America's simple common courtesy.** The "Hi!" coming from anyone passing my way, even from total strangers, is wonderful. In the words of an American philosopher whose name I don't recall: "Simple courtesy and its secret ingredient, humor, are the necessary glues to hold society together." Isn't that a great maxim?
- **"Johnny Appleseed," the folk tale.** I imagine him in his "heavenly orchard" whenever I see a blossoming apple tree.
- **America's bountiful supply of food.** In this country, you can find and eat any food that Mother Earth produces, about any time, independently of the season.
- **The ACLU (American Civil Liberties Union).**
- **Creators of children's movies in Hollywood.** Fun and frolic loving, they produce movies with no PG or X ratings—as of now.
- **Virginia's glorious Luray Caverns.** Indeed, the caverns are some of the most beautiful caves in the world. I also love other less-frequented places like **Hiawasee,** in Georgia, and square dancing in **Cheyenne Wyoming** (this German gets around!); **Kings Mountain** in North Carolina— The battle fought here in 1780 destroyed the left wing of the British army and effectively ended Loyalist ascendance in the Carolinas during the Revolutionary War—**Austin, Texas**, for its clean waters, **Montauk, New York** for its breezing morning sun, the "**Arizona Sonora Desert Museum," and the rural back roads of Maryland, Pennsylvania, West Virginia, Colorado, California**—yes, there are still hidden off-the-coast roads there—and other places in the U.S. of magic and wonder from **the Grand Canyon** to **the beaches of Emerald Isle in the Carolinas;**
- **Unedited, live TV shows** like those spelling bees with the question, "How do you spell relief?" and the surprise answer (I am not making this up) "F-A-R-T" by a smart nine-year-old boy.

- **Words of peace**. There are few uttered words, hardly discernible, of peace. They should be heard much more than the loud yells of bellicose terms coming from high places.
- **America's innumerable volunteers**—in all fields, especially in theaters and soup kitchens, silently contributing to the minds and health of this country without compensation.
- **The Smithsonian Institution** with its vast educational programs on about any and all fields of cultural occupation.
- **Environmentally conscious persons,** who fight an uphill battle against the government's big business interest groups in order to preserve what Nature (still) offers us.
- **Black Baptist churches.** I enjoy the sheer exultation I find in these churches—the only truly jubilant expression of faith, so it seems to me, a man without religious preference.
- **The devotion of teachers and librarians.** Their plain goals are to pass on what they have learned, experienced, and know to future generations. "The progress of humanity lies solely in what we pass on to others," according to my late mentor, Jean Lurçat. **The fighters,** who still, vaguely, try to establish the only forgotten one of the Human Rights: the Right To Be Different. Oh my, now the Supreme Court's closet doors will shut for good.
- **Hay mazes and hay rides.** For me, these take place in private orchards and farms opened to the public "during the season." To be young again—there I do feel young.
- **The altruistic care of nurses.**
- **The general hospitality of the South**—where life is lived less hectically and often less selfishly than in the North.
- **The enormous variety of opinions**—leftover remnants of "freedom of speech," if you will, in countless local papers and other media.
- **Pecan pies and corn on the cob and plantains** (unknown in Europe), and treats coming from the heart.

- **The absence of formality** in museums. Polite requests of museum directors to address them by their first name, dropping titles of doctor or professor are absolutely unheard of in Europe, especially in mountainous Austria.
- **Halloween mania.** I am amused by the All-Hallows antics of my kids and all other American youngsters.
- **Plum butter**, and **some of the homemade breads**—that do not in the least remind me of the chewing gum-like bread in the fast food joints.
- **California wines** and, in moderation, the finest **Appalachian distilleries**.
- **Art exhibitions mounted at the National Gallery of Art**—some never to be forgotten, for example, the "1492-1992" show, the "Olmecs" or the exhibit on "Imperial China," and many smaller exhibits, turning the least interested visitors into art enthusiasts.
- **Untreated apples a**nd **broccoli a**nd really **sweet potatoes** and **Fadley's crab cakes** in Baltimore.
- **Amusement parks** when they are closed.
- **The National Mall in D.C.** I am finding far less fast food debris than I had feared; and the **National Arboretum**—hello, Micah, "arbor" is Latin for "tree."
- **Neighbors** who replace their gas-guzzling suv's with cars and those who recycle (a tiny minority, unfortunately) and the few, the proud, the very few good plumbers whose work turns out to be reliable even after several weeks.
- Little old Jewish ladies of "Leisure World" who have a way with "highbrow" words and wit.
- **All of you who are not (yet) addicted to TV soaps** or the Internet or computer games and such distractions.
- **Reading American poets and other authors,** for example, James Michener, or Robert Frost, or Howard Lyman *(Mad Cowboy*, a must for all vegans).
- **Performances** and the enriching, touching, thrilling concerts at the Kennedy Center's Concert Hall.

- **Swimming in the Atlantic Ocean** and **the Pacific Ocean off the California coast** "in winter," when the locals take pictures of me because I'm swimming in their ocean at below 60 degrees (the Baltic Sea is colder and more refreshing, I'm telling you).
- Off-Broadway theaters and the expressions of talent and artistic ideas found in these small, unknown, unsupported theaters.
- **Sitcoms**, if their jokes make the slightest sense.
- **Living and moving here freely**—and I know of formidable, hidden places most U.S. citizens have never even heard of.
- **What the Statue of Liberty stands for**: the very personal liberties Americans enjoy and experience daily, keep the country *liber*, save the liberties. Cheers!

And now back to our interrupted field trip. My musing in broad daylight comes to an abrupt end; it is time to begin the return trip, after Eric rushed again to the bathroom and after Buddy made a not-so-funny remark about the farm ("Not everything that grows naturally is natural.") and after Molly reminded us, the adults, that the only students invited on the next field trip should be the ones who promise to eat the fresh fruit and vegetables. Then we'd only need a car and not a bus.

Just to irritate us, Mrs. Glut brings us back to the topic of our detour and second unplanned stop with this mouthful.

"The French taste buds with their refined nerves are considered to rank number two in the world, right after the Chinese, who enjoy eating rotten eggs, among other things. I am dying to know how this much-celebrated *gourmand* ..."— she tries her tongue in the French language, which is evidently not hers—"will react to his very first American hamburger."

So am I, but for different reasons. She has the say here. Had she recommended a detour via the South Pole, we would have had to follow her there, too. Gnashing our teeth, we have no choice but to take in everything else she has to tell us about this illustrious chef.

"This world-class chef received not four, but five stars in the latest Michelin Guide. Imagine that—five! When such an expert from the land of delicacy and taste comes to us, it must ..."

"Mean something?" Mr. Darkbeer bluntly interrupts. "I don't think so. And it is also doubtful whether la France deserves your gourmet ranking. It is possible to eat as well and as delicately in Hungary, India, in Holland or Norway and Sweden, or Singapore and more civilly and at more reasonable prices."

"And in Italy," Miss Watchout adds.

"And in Latin America," opines Mrs. Solidario.

"Japanese cuisine is also quite something," is my modest contribution, not to mention my favoring of the good old home cooking of Germany. Sauerkraut is not the daily meal there.

"I'm hungry!" moans Chief.

Again the children are rollicking about on the school bus. We adults had best devote our attention to calming the kids down.

"A song, anybody?" I ask, but harvest only laughter. No one wants to sing; bawling is simply more fun. Besides advertising jingles, the youth of today know little else.

"Drive faster! Faster!" Mack yells from far back in the bus and he is applauded for it.

The two classes are eager for the upcoming event with the anticipated TV fuss, as each kid imagines what might be in it for him or her. Slowly we are approaching the scene of the glorious propaganda idea. On both sides of the street we see parked cars and a whole lot of police in cars, on horses, on foot, and on motorcycles. In front of the fast food place many still photographers are taking flash photographs of the scenery. The TV crews have all eyes on the limo of the distinguished guest from Europe, who is just about to get out of his rented luxury car. The police guide us to a reserved space of the parking lot and we are asked not to leave the bus yet.

Thunderclouds are rapidly forming and it is getting darker. We arrive just in time to see a storm of flashing lights welcoming the French five-star chef—here only "to taste a bit of something typically American," as Mrs. Glut puts it. The man in the gray flannel is ugly as sin. Even the hunchback of Nôtre Dame would have had little chance against him. He looks as though he fell out of an airplane. To compensate for his own lack of a good figure, he is in company of three extremely beautiful, shapely women I presume to be models, who know exactly how to draw the attention of all the cameramen to them. The three are putting on a spectacular show, shielding the man in gray.

"I'm hungry," Samantha calls out again to my dismay.

We all laugh, but then we are as overawed as the large crowd outside and start gaping in reverence and in an unusual silence.

The parade into the food-facility begins. What a show! Only the Pope's procession must have more dignity. Yet, after less than two minutes, the three smiling beauties return—alone. Their rules for slimness obviously do not allow the intake of fat meat. Our group in the bus and the people in the parking lot, and many more curious folks flocking to this scene are on high alert to see what might happen when the door opens again and the five-star guest gives his much-anticipated commentary on American food for the purpose of the new advertising campaign. We are to be witnesses. What painful torment to make us wait so long. What will the highly praised man of refined senses choose for his exquisite wording? How many million more hamburgers will Mcdonald's sell due to his singular expression of European taste? Who could be the next stars from overseas in line and how much will they cash in? The tension grows. Is he making eyes at the cooking arts of this restaurant famous for counting its sales not in millions but in billions? What ...?

There…now… a commotion at the door, bathed in a sea of spotlights. Suddenly the high priest of modern cuisine stumbles out of the eatery, all pale, ashen. He staggers and his three beauties catch him just before he collapses. How terrible! How unexpected! He has passed out. Then the incomprehensible happens—he comes to and has a shivering fit. He shudders with disgust and then does it—he starts to vomit. The very sight is revolting. He continues to throw up. No, he pukes his guts out. How horrible! To our surprise, the TV teams turn their cameras away from the sickening scene and do not film it. Of all things! Isn't any TV crew famous for reporting the "sensational," especially when it borders on the grotesque, the revolting, the absurd, and the unappetizing scenes of this sick world? Why not here? Orders from their superiors? Or do they need to turn their heads away so as not to throw up themselves? We are disappointed.

Mr. Droldegout finally stands up awkwardly and finds his composure. All attention is again focusing on him and now he delivers his first and last statement on American soil.

"I would have to be either half-starved, or extremely stupid to rush in and out of such a fast food place. It tastes simply horrible. That food is—in one word—hideous. I propose a new motto for this hamburger chain, which, I deeply regret to admit, conquers the entire globe in an advertisement bonanza of unknown dimensions and at outrageous costs. And my motto for them is ..."

He belches, while we all hold our breath.

**"Eat Now, Throw Up Later!"**

Without even a goodbye, he is rushed away in his limo. His blunt remarks were not reported in the U.S., but for sure in France, where the whole population was shrieking with laughter.

Our Buddy rhymes happily, "The greatest cook from France ... made a mess in his pants ...!"

# Epilogue

Now, wasn't that a stunning surprise? Will Macdonald's sue me now for reporting the unfriendly incident? Did this fine gentleman get paid in advance and will the burger producers demand their investment back for... slander and defamation? Great questions, indeed. I hear someone laughing and beg that person to be quiet for a while, as it gets serious again. All of us on the bus, teachers, chaperons and the poor children, who fell silent from disgust and astonishment—with the exception, perhaps, of Mrs. Glut—have lost any appetite for a hamburger from that food chain. Oh, how I would love to shout out after the creator of the advertisement flop, "*Au revoir, Monsieur Droldegout.* ('Goodbye, Mr. Oddtaste') Are you now going to knock down all the Macdonald's on the Champs-Elysées and elsewhere in la belle France? If so, do you need a hand?"

Our field trip to the Merryland Farm had brought us much joy and satisfaction, nothing evil happened until we returned to this place. The kids truly regret not having eaten some fruits from the orchard now that they will not eat here and have to witness how this famed chef is emptying himself in the glare of TV lights. Maybe the first burger he tasted went down the wrong way? Who knows? Or, is it possible that his fine inner eyes showed him flickering images of the filth and the horror scenes that are daily routines in the slaughterhouses? Whatever.

For all of you who rush to the fast food chains on a routine basis, this secluded world of the slaughtering with the torture, blood, death and disgust, the mass slaying of cows, chicken, and sheep does not exist, or does it? You call reports about it "sensationalism." You close your eyes and for you these animals are surely sitting golden-brownish broiled on their neat heaps of aseptic manure, aren't they? Well, they don't.

Allow me to steal this pretty picture from you and let me disturb your peace filled with smacking sounds a little bit. Let me wake you meat-devourers up and turn your attention to the horrible reality behind the yummy facades. Or should I wait till one of you has a little mishap like the connoisseur from Lyon?

It is a sad truth that the much-celebrated "food pyramid" for a healthy diet stands upside down in the U.S. The base should be grain, then the vegetable, then fruit, only then the meat and fat and sugar at the very top. It is the opposite here and no one regrets it. (The weight-loss industry, of course, is happy about it.) How can we reverse this order? I believe that only a radical cure may save the country from going totally obese ...

Let us contemplate this: If the fattening (the extra-feeding, including dead animals) of the cattle could be banned and if most (not all) flesh eaters were to turn vegetarian (temporarily), there would be reason for jubilation, but *pia desideria* (pious wishes). Yet, to simply start a new nationwide diet program, wouldn't it be thinkable for those lusting for hamburgers (the addicts) to give up their habit once a week or at least once a month and if even that is "too often," to introduce one flesh-free day a year as a National Healthfood Day (no work). This would mean that Macdonald's and other fast food chains would have to close their doors for one whole day. Such a closing is unthinkable, unheard of, and definitely inconceivable because of the loss of profile and of profit. The meat industry lobby and its suppliers, and investors will pull all tricks to avert such a catastrophic assault on their income and will end any debate in Congress before it even starts. So, it will remain only an idea.

If it continues, if obesity becomes the number one health problem of the nation, if more rainforests are cleared to make space for more grazing land for more cattle in order to keep up with the ever-growing demand for more meat ("I'm hungry!"), and if the seats in cars and airplanes have to be adjusted so that the potbellied passengers can sit comfortably (this is no joke), and when the rain becomes scarce in the Midwest (the nation's granary) because of ecological structure changes (due to deforestation), and when finally an endless drought devastates ranches and fields, when cattle have to be destroyed, and the meat must be dumped, and the methods and habits of fast fat eating must change, and when Wall Street figures fall and fall, maybe then we will wake up and rub our piggish eyes and remind ourselves of healthier nutrition and better ways of life, independent of the daily bombardment in the media commercials with their motto, "Eat until you burst." Maybe then we might realize that the meat eaters, apart from their grunting sounds, are slowly approaching their sacrificed animals visually as well. Is that a rotten trick of Mother Nature's revenge? No, it is our very own fault as the result of our very own unwillingness to change.

Until this realization sets foot in our brains, a lot more trash has to be removed from the brains of those who stubbornly and vehemently refuse to learn what is indeed behind the stuff they desire and what is in the fast food that they swallow **without question, without shame, and without a second thought.**

Suddenly, Micah's voice interrupts my musing,

"Papa, tomorrow we're going back to our local Macdonald's right after school, will you join us? Pleeeease?"

I take a very deep breath and sigh. "Phew!" Swell. Cheers then!

# 9-11-2001

The often humorous and ironic tone of my writings in the German edition of *I Hate Junk Food* have been altered in this English edition because of the somber, sad, and tragic events of September 11, 2001. A consequence of that fateful day and its horrors has been a continuous rise in anti-Arab sentiment throughout the U.S.

Most of us still shudder, clench our fists, grind our teeth, or shiver with anger and disgust when recalling 9-11-2001. We lost a part of our "feel-good" habits—forever. Yet, the question must be addressed: Why did it happen?

There are American voices stating that "the alliance with Israel was the main cause for the terrorist attacks" in New York, Virginia, and Pennsylvania.

We all abhor the terror of the suicide bombers in Israel, but we must look for an answer to the question "Why?"

## 1

An American citizen, a Palestinian-American lady, gave me the answer to President Bush's question: "Why do they [the Arabs] hate us? Quite simply: because of his 101 percent pro-Israel policies." (She cannot be labeled an "anti-Semite" because, as a Palestinian, she is a Semite herself.)

# 2
# Ashes to Ashes

Bright morning light hits the World Trade Center towers.
On floor 100, a thoughtful trader to his young assistant:
"Wonderful ideas are coming to my head, and you know what?
Before I sort them out, I might be dead... And tomorrow? I
wished for my last years to simply live spaciously and
graciously and nothing more, see, nothing more." She smiles at
him and starts to say: "Don't we all..." Suddenly, a shadow,
the attack, the explosion. Both vanish. Floors burning, bending,
caving in, then crumbling to ashes, to dust, to nothing more but
ashes.

Overheard by survivors, voices of the falling victims:
"Help! Terror, fear, flames and no escape, evil and death.
Ashes, the horror, screams, anguish, black clothes, and fire."

Engulfed in smoke and dust, a lost, fleeing group, ashen faces:
"Farewell my life, farewell this world,
farewell tears, touch, and soft embrace.
Farewell memory and kisses, farewell peace,
farewell all mercy, prayers, sunshine, and grace.
Farewell my love, farewell sweet light,
farewell tall city and farewell all pain,
and joy and help and day and night.
Farewell hushed voices, bliss, and tender care,
and welcome silence, death, eternal rest and..."

Nothing more, just horror and nothing more.
Ashes, fading cries, and nothing more... nothing.

# 3
# Christmas Letter to the Author, 2001

GOD
BLESS
~~AMERICA~~
THE WORLD

>IRK —

What a year! One that has forever changed the lives of every person living on this planet. 9/11 will always be remembered as the day we got slapped "up-side the head" and realized we are not so big, powerful, and isolated from the rest of the world like we have always thought. We can no longer believe we are so much better than other humans on Earth...that we can ignore their low standard of living and suffering while we bask in our pampered and excess material world called the USA.

It bugs me to still see all this "national pride" going on everywhere with flags flying and our President saying "God bless America" with every second statement. This is exactly the mindset that got us into this mess in the first place. "I am amazed that people would hate us," remarked President Bush, "because I know how good we are." A discourse that casts the American role in the world as simply "good" and acknowledges none of our own self-interest brutalities and past exploitations is a bit naive.

This attitude isn't just American however. Throughout history, most major wars were caused by or fought (and still are) over religion. "God is on our side therefor we are right...even if we have to kill in the name of God." How misconstrued this thinking is. Hate and killing "in the name of God" is an oxymoron. Yet here we go again. Replaying the same old record. God represents love, compassion, and kindness and all the other beautiful qualities of life. Anything else represents the opposite of God. The fact that there are dozens of religions doesn't matter. All are praying to the same God while going through similar yet uniquely different lifetime experiences on earth. To think one is any better (or the only way) is such archaic thinking. All are on the same path and destiny. All are praying to the same God even if they use different languages and call "God" by another name. As long as we believe the old mindset, we will continue to have wars and conflicts on Earth. RON

# 4
# New Year's Letter to the Author, 2002

Dear Mr. Holger,

In sending you our greetings at the end of a calamitous year, we cannot separate our thoughts from the events of September 11th and our sense of their profound significance for the future of the world. In 1996, Renée-Marie wrote an article for *The Human Quest* under the title "The Root Causes of Terrorism and the Only Way to Stop It." Its prophetic relevance was such that the editors of *The Human Quest* chose to print the same article again in their current November/December issue. It has thus been quite a few years that we have lived in expectation of some such horrific, climactic disaster!

You may perhaps agree that in the short term, terrorism cannot be defeated. For much too long the policies of the rich nations have failed to address—and often caused!—the vast majority on our planet. While the rich got richer, the poor have gotten poorer, giving rise to growing resentment, hate, and finally—in desperation—to bloody instincts of retribution and to a vicious cycle of revenge. The Palestinians' tragedy, the persecution and massacre of the Kurds, the suffering and deaths of the Iraqi people, and now the terror experienced by the hapless millions of Afghans fleeing from bombs and starvation, weigh down on our hearts. The long-term remedy lies surely in a committed and enduring drive for economic and social justice on a global scale. We continue to hope against hope that the catastrophic events of 2001 and their aftermath will, at long last, change the minds of governments to improve radically the human condition on our planet. How we wish we were fifty years younger to join our energies to the efforts of so many organizations that attempt to deal with this tragic state of affairs. We cannot help but share in the enormous guilt of present generations to have created such gigantic problems for those who will have to cope when we are gone...

√ the plight of ...

To tell you of our own work and experience in this context might appear almost trivial, though we have had in fact another active year whose highlights we would like to share with you…

R.M.-P.H Florida

# 5
# Intifada

Anybody who is unable to see a connection between the Israeli occupation of Arab lands and the events of 9-11-01 should skip this and read the next story.

In 1991, I wrote a short play on the first "Intifada" (the Palestinian uprising against the Israeli oppression) to lend a voice to those who have no voice in the U.S. It was not a documentary, but was entirely based on facts. Who could envision that the Israeli occupation and the Palestinian refugee camps with their horrible living conditions would last another decade?

I wanted to include the play in this book, but was vehemently warned by my American relatives and friends not to do so, or else I would be targeted as an "anti-Semite" and thus would be silenced, or worse. Since such groups as the Jewish (not "Semitic") Defense League (JDL), or the American Israel Public Affairs Committee (AIPAC) have great influence on both the U.S. Government and the media, I heeded their warnings (So much for "freedom of speech" in this country!). With the second Intifada now raging, I think it is time to do some semantics: if one is pro-Palestinian, one should not be labeled as an "anti-Semite," as the Palestinians *are* Semites. Instead, I would prefer to be called a "pro-Semite," although it looks as if this noble word has not even been coined yet.

G.W. Bush asked, "Why do they [the Arabs] hate us?" He got a very short, straight answer written on a poster during a rare pro-Palestinian (pro-Semite?) demonstration in Washington, D.C.:

**"It's the Occupation, Stupid!"**

(Of course, nobody denies Israel's right to exist, but not at the expense of Palestinian statehood.)

And here I will quote yet another American voice, so far unheard: "As the Palestinians are Semites in their vast majority, while the Israelis are Semites only in a small minority, those who are protesting the ongoing Israeli occupation of the West Bank and Gaza, with all the humiliation and dehumanization of the defenseless Palestinians cannot be branded 'anti-Semites.' This term is being used as a weapon on everyone who speaks his or her mind about Israel's policies: ignoring U.N. resolutions on the illegal Jewish settlements, [Israel's] official assassination politics, and its continuing to degrade an occupied people without arms to defend itself. The tragic result is the 'suicide bomber' with his or her horrific actions. Nobody is allowed to talk about the only solution: when the (American-sponsored) occupation ends, the Intifada and with it the suicide bombings will end. Period. This, of course, is a pro-Semitic statement, but it will surely be branded as 'anti-Semitic' rhetoric by those who still believe in Israel's superiority. As the World Trade Center towers fell, so too will this doomed policy, and I am not the only one in the Western world who sees it that way…"

This is—word for word—the view of a concerned U.S. citizen, who wishes to remain anonymous, but I am allowed to give her initials: H.A. (No, dear reader, not Dr. Hannan Ashrawi. Her voice will, hopefully, be more listened to in the future, worldwide to include the United States of America. At least, this is my no-longer-secret wish)

# 6
# The Vigil, or Am I an American?

A month after the terrible events of 9-11-2001, on a warm autumn evening in Olney, at first a few neighbors, then more and more walked with lit candles in their hands out to the corner of Hines Road and Macduff Avenue—a spontaneous vigil in remembrance of the victims of the terror attacks in New York, Virginia, and Pennsylvania. While the kids played with the flickering candles, the adults formed small groups to share their feelings and to free themselves of their profound thoughts about the tragedy. When a Filipino lady, a young mother with some ten members of her family present, mentioned that she knew one of the victims and started to cry, I could not hold back my emotions and cried, too.

"You knew someone who died there, too?" asked a beautifully dressed, elegant black lady, a neighbor from a few blocks down the road.

"No," I replied. "I didn't know anyone. And I'm not even an American."

She hugged me and said, "But tonight, see, in your heart, you *are* an American."

# Christmas, New York Style

Eggnog alone didn't do the trick, so we had whiskey as well to warm us up. It was cold indeed in the city's twilight, as it got darker. Happily drunk, we staggered through this "Holy Night" somewhere in downtown New York City in the 1970s. The exact year is forgotten, but not the curious events of that night.

Longing for the warmth and Christmas decorations at Lillian's apartment, we felt heavenly despite the cold. We easily shrugged off the streets' unduly loud noises, already calmer than usual. It was as if a wondrous spell of silent joy had fallen over the normally bustling city. Even the air was filled with a quiet feeling of something "holy." The three of us—the big "D's:" Dennis, Dick, and Dirk—slowly slipped into a blessed Christmas Eve spirit. Snowflakes danced around us. We looked at each other, and at the tall buildings wrapped in the stillness of this special night, and we realized that we ought to be ashamed of our drunken behavior.

As we got closer to Lillian's place, we started to hum "Silent night, holy night/all is calm/all is ..." and cried. Our mood, helped along with a little booze, was joyful, festive. Clutching elaborately wrapped gifts, we were overwhelmed by a magical and celebratory spirit. Our humming stopped. All was quiet.

Suddenly, and unwanted, a voice from a dark corner intruded: "Drugs, anyone? Speed? Ups or downs? Green light? Wanna get high?"

Disgusted, we hurried on, but as we approached the "Women's Tower," infamous then, gone today, we regained our festive mood and began to sing again this night's song of songs, but now louder so that those poor imprisoned souls up there in the Tower could hear us. To our delight, at first a few voices, then more and more female voices came from the countless Tower windows singing with us. Passers-by stopped, stayed with us, and sang the enchanting hymn, too. And like us, they looked up with moist eyes to the unseen prisoners. Thoughts of grace, and blessing, and wonder filled our heads. As we sang one Christmas song after another, we came to the beautiful line: "And may all your Christmases be white."

The voices sounding from the Tower quickly turned vulgar and began shrieking obscenities.

Enraged, the other onlookers-turned-carolers stalked off shaking their fists at the unseen women cursing them. Curses on Christmas Eve? Well, we were in Manhattan where anything is possible at any time.

Shocked, we—the three Ds—burst into laughter. The ugly Tower voices stopped ... and then joined in laughter.

Was it a ruined Christmas Eve? If I were to tell you the complete chronology of what followed on that both wonderful and strange night, I guarantee you would slap this book around my ears. Therefore, I keep this mixed memory of a memorable night in New York to myself and remain silent.

Anyway, shortly after midnight, a blizzard-like snowstorm blanketed the entire city. Piling up snow to incredible heights. The falling white veil hushed all but our inner voices—and those were glorious.

# Poetical Thoughts

## 1

### The World's End
### (Robert Frost's "Fire and Ice" in mind)

The world will neither
end in fire,
nor will it end
in ice.

It passes by
its well-deserved pyre
and is on its way
to slow demise.

The world's inhabitants
are mad and maddening,
their lives, their fates
are sad and saddening.

This world is
rotting away
to a cursed
and painful, dark decay.

And when it's time
it does one last leap
unsung on the Cosmos' own,
forgotten dung heap.

But then again,
even there is life
and a better new world
will start and thrive!

## 2

### Gorgon Dreams

Late at night, amidst sleeping rocks and fossils,
under a moonless sky, weaponless, naked, but fearless, I lie.
Thrown into this cold darkness, where no living soul should
roam,
I see her rising, there, on the tallest one of the nightly cliffs,
the mortal one of the Gorgons, facing me, petrifyingly,
with such a horrible gaze that I want to turn my head.
Instead, I recollect all memories and strength
and stare right back. "Who will turn whom to stone?"
I shout into the shadows, where all sounds are deadened
except the voice of courage. "Who has to fear whom?"
A first, faint shiver starts building up, I tremble…
When suddenly, invisibly, yet fully there,
I get a hold of Perseus' sword,
passed on to me by unknown forces.
I raise my hand, I raise my arm, I hesitate.
Late at night I must decide
whether to conquer fear and fight.
Quickly I make up my mind, I rest my arm,
I drop the sword and I am asking: "Why?"
"Why fight a ghost of the past, gone for millennia?"
In facing her alone lies my survival, in knowing her,
not in destroying the mortal Gorgon.
Let Medusa's snakes keep hissing on.
Late at night I have decided not to fear, and not to fight.

I end my ghostly Gorgon dream and turn on the light.

## 3

### *In Memoriam*, Alice Hawthorne
### (Atlanta Olympics, 1996)

While the Olympic flame, extinguished now,
will burn again in a few years,
your radiant smile was never buried.
Nor was your Guardian Angel asleep that night
when an explosive fire lit the Atlanta sky
to seal your fate.

Instead, it seems to me as if you just passed by
to sprinkle rosebud seeds all over the world.
And, whenever I again touch a night rose,
your memory,
I then will know that a Holy Thorn,
its spirit and its essence,
lies beneath the wondrous surface:
your unforgettable face,
your unforgettable fate,

your dream,

your life.

# 4

## Out of my Shadow Into Light

Bewildering mystery awakes in me, stirs up my quietude.
My eyes are burning as in dreams, my ears
cannot define the remote sound—a blue
song of farewell and of welcome, too,
in unheard melody and in hushed whisper.
"Love leaves all grief behind," it says.
Angels taking measure and they sing—my reverie,
once filled with sadness, ends in jubilation.
I hear a song of rapture in exultant tones,
on shiftless waves of air it swings.
I hear the subtle sound of a hidden door being opened,
I see a fable's fabric discoloring itself—for me,
deflowering my dreamlike veneration.
Fair indeed is the beckoning of idea's radiance.
To this arresting symptom of new passion I respond.
Hearsay, in its own shadow, sits in judgment, lost.
Afraid anew of afterthoughts and tears,
I dig my heart out and I realize:
Bright evidence displays a faint omen
to guard and shield what lives in me unharmed,
a lustrous, yes, imposing, fame:
The splendor of my heart, I must admit,
is occupied by an enchantress!
Her name is endless, so it seems:
It is delight and charm, comfort and care,
enrapture, august joy, and blissful hysteria,
auspice and harmony, magnificence, and ecstasy!
It is resplendent glory, devoted fascination,
enticing love and, yes, it is
bewildering mystery!

I wake up, I am daydreaming and I smile.

# 5
## Come Furnish Me with a Laugh

Somewhere out of the burning sky, a brilliant
thought floats towards me. Looking up,
all senses alert, I see a copper circle shining
bright and red fire. I rub my eyes; it is
a good luck penny tossed in the air by little hands
and picked up happily by my little one. He catches it,
no, I catch it with my heart, the copper-red thought fades.

Mine was the copper thought, too red, too hot,
too sparkling to be caught and kept. I drop it.
The air is hot and waves of heat drift up the air
I breathe. Two naked little hands pull with a smile
the clouds of doubt away from me.
In the blue air, I doze off, away to another country,
without fear. With spring fountains, birds, and with
good people who love each other and who care.
This foreign place is paradise and boring.
My little boy is with me here while I am snoring!

# 6

## The Young Fiddler On the Rock

(I listened to some "News of the Time"
and took the liberty of putting them in rhyme)
The young fiddler of Doolin,
so the saying goes,
threw himself off
the staggering cliffs
of storm-ridden Moher.
That was on Mother's Day
some two hundred years ago.
Today, the Doolin Ferry
still travels over his bones,
buried in the salty sea.
He was no Catholic soul,
so he was soon forgotten.
But his spirited ghost
still lingers in the breezing air
over the sea and barren coast.
He loathed his fellows' relaxed way
of normal living, and
having no other faith but in himself,
he took his life into his own hands
and jumped off the cliffs that sad day.
An eerie murmur can be heard
from time to time on foggy nights
when the sea is calm.
And a high-pitched tone as well,
resounding from the middle cliffs.
It is there where his fiddle landed

when the saddened dream of his life ended.

# 7

## Rose Without Thorn

Rose without thorn
Unicorn without horn
Dawn without breath
Life without death
Time without hour
Thought without power
Might without order
World without border
Air without cloud
Being without doubt
Day without night
Fate without plight
Night without shadow
Dream without meadow
Love without pain
End without name

Unicorn without horn
Rose without thorn

# 8
## Quatrains
## *In Memoriam*, Omar Khayyam (1050-1123)

Pouring the pleasures of wine, to shine,
into his colorful quatrains, forbidden wine,
the fabled tentmaker, not an ascetic,
sagacious Omar Khayyam, sets minds poetic.

Whoever enjoyed high ecstasies,
has shared the wine of his sagacity.
Rose petals come with the North wind's blaze,
fill Khayyam's grave with august amaze!

———————

Love is the most powerful
motive for murder.
Please, don't tell me that
you really love me to death!

———

We live in the space age
with the brain of the Stone Age: tough!
Decoding our social clues we find:
Being normal these days is crazy enough!

# 9

The darkest spirits
cast the longest shadows.
Avert your eyes from evil!
Walk instead in flowering meadows!

---

An endless flood of tears
drowns pain and sorrow.
The Earth is a burial place,
today and tomorrow.

---

The chosen ones are always those
who suffer the most, tearless.
In pain-wracked bodies develops
the chosen soul, fearless.

---

We do not just die to end
our terrestrial journey,
but to find out
where it started.

---

To the mailbox she walks cheerfully,
from the mailbox she returns tearfully.
"Something wrong?" I ask Miss Melanie Mills.
"No, she replies, I'm just allergic to bills!"

---

"Modern times are just a curse!"
swears the pickpocket, and takes off
with the little old lady under his arm
who wouldn't let go of her purse.

# GERMAN TALES

# The Bathtub of the Holy Joseph

Anyone who loves to share a laugh when recollecting the "fun, fat, felt, and frolic" art period in West Germany after World War II remembers with either delight, or derision, the famous "bathtub" story. This is a true account of that notorious art affair.

Joseph, our kind and good-natured friend, took his art piece—bathtub—all the way to the Leverkusen Museum so that the masses could better understand the visual arts. He was not at all upset when his mentor, a museum director, told him that someone had actually scrubbed his curious art object.

He did call the museum. "Wonderful! Just great! Who had that splendid idea? It's cleaned? Now it is again pure, clean art and no single bloody person can curse my art as greasy or grimy or filthy or what-have-you. Heavenly! Who did it? Who? Impossible! Say it again! A cleaning lady from your own museum! In my bathtub? Are you crazy or am I going nuts? A simple woman showed an understanding of my art and purified it? Superb! There you see how far I've come with my lectures on broadening the concepts of art all the way down to commoners, the cleaning people. Now I can take a bath again in my old, rotten tub, fabulous. These are still times for a miracle, even in Germany. Is the tub not only clean, but also truly white again?"

The rest of this curiosity is well-documented and known to all lovers of modern art. A tribunal was started: What was the art here? A claim for compensation by the museum was to answer the burning question of an entire nation: Was the elimination of dirt an act of damage to an art object? Is someone laughing?

The real fun and laughter began when art perverts offered as generous donations their own dirty bathtubs and unclean toilets in newspaper ads throughout the country. "Must genuine German art really have to be filthy?" was a headline in one German newspaper.

The greatest outpouring of sympathy for the poor artist, canonized already by art critics, came after the high court's verdict. The court awarded 60,000 DM as damages and that was not a juicy morsel; it was an insult—a mere half of what the art-tub was appraised and acquired for. Did his efforts on behalf of "art for the common man" get a slap in the face? Was the honor of post-war German art blemished, or was it saved? Who else, besides the "greatest living German artist of the 20th century" had profited from the court's action?

Here is the verdict, word for word: "It is not the bathtub by itself that is a work of art; rather, the fact that the master [without quotation marks] has touched it with his [greasy] hand has turned the tub into a work of art." Period. Poor German art, or poor bathtub, to end up in the trade for devotional objects!

*Post Scriptum*—As all other unfinished things, this revealing story has its sequel, too. A photo document shows a bathtub hanging by its single pipe from the only remaining wall of a house in Wuppertal that had been bombed out in an air raid in 1943. Its owner, Dr. Heinrich Hahne, who happened to be my former Latin professor and who was the underdog in the St. Joseph lawsuit, tried hard to convince the court that his tub might have both a higher value in terms of art history as well as political and cultural history than the one that had been scrubbed by Erna Bosomjoy of the Leverkusen museum. Unfortunately, his tub lacked the magic touch by the "master" and hence remained just what it was—scrap. Pity.

# Death Of A Great (?) Singer

In the time of the Reich that we refer to as the "Third," a highly regarded general lived in cabaret-crazy Berlin, the capital of the "Third" Reich. He had won his high regard in the Prussian military and in many drink-happy singing clubs. One beautiful day, on invitations printed on the finest handmade paper, he invited his fellow party members as well as friends and family to a memorial service for a "great singer who has just passed away." For whom? Guesses were made and many names were whispered, but no one dared, out of respect for the capacity of the general's family to mourn, to inquire about the identity of the deceased.

On the day of the wake, mourners dressed in black, and some others in an even blacker black, assemble in a stately home darkened by crêpe arranged discreetly in the pattern of a swastika. Shortly after the mourners arrival, glasses are distributed filled with hard liquor. The initial solemn stillness recedes and makes room for an almost detached mood around the unusually high catafalque festooned with black velvet and sitting in the middle of the main hall of the general's villa.

The lady of the great house, apparently already somewhat tipsy, smoothes out wrinkles in the shroud, but suddenly breaks out in heavy sobs as a particularly thick-headed Hitler Youth member sings, "Along flew a bird, and landed on my grave ..." The general helps his wife, close to fainting, stand up, and the entire assembly holds its breath as he announces, "Let us now say our final farewells to my dearest friend, whose song even brought joy to (hic) the Pope when he once heard him sing. It was far and away the most beautiful voice. The most divine (hic) voice (hic) ..."

The newly refilled glasses have a sadness-negating effect, even on the military personnel.

"...that ever was heard in our house or at the party headquarters where I would often take him along on the days of victory celebrations."

Thereupon, a great lady from the Berliner aristocracy cries out: "Cheers!" Quite a few faces with glassy eyes turn to stare at her. So, she helps herself to another drink.

The lady of the house, completely disoriented and disconnected, turns to her husband, "Imagine that I have lost my hearing from sadness and pain. That is the heaviness of my heart after the loss of our dear, dear friend. Why are we being punished with his untimely death, do you know?" She sobs heartbreakingly.

The general begins to blubber: how very unGerman of him. "Only heaven knows (hic). Now, since the sweetest voice in our house is forever silent, what will become of our future without him?"

His distraught wife replies, "Heaven, dearest, heaven is his place from now on. Heaven will give us a sign. I will keep my faith to the last. He, he'll come again, won't he? No music, my love, can be spectacular enough to accompany our silenced friend to the eternal fields far above our earthly existence, none except our national anthem? Let it fly high into the endless heavens, fly up, my dear little soul!"

Naturally, he tries to comfort her. "Whenever a cloud passes by, the cloud will (hic) start to sing and we (hic), we will hear him sing through the cloud."

The next question from his wife has an almost sobering effect. "Do we have enough wine, schnapps, and champagne? Remember how much the guests at our last wake drank up? It's strange to think that the mourners at our house are always so thirsty. It's as if they had been dry the whole year. They come, get away with a few tears, and then seem to be completely dried out and whoosh, they all mob the bar and ..."

"Hit the booze!" her husband continues.

"They drink so much you wonder if they want to drown the reason for such a sad occasion."

The general adds, "They're washing the (hic) reason for their grief down the drain, as they say."

"Well," inquires Madame: "Do we have enough this time? I'm worried that…"

He sees no need to let her finish. "Don't worry, dearest (hic), I've invited both of the Lollies and they're (hic) bringing the usual replenishment along."

"What? Not those crazy Lollies, of all people."

"Yes," he affirms. "Today they are coming to mourn and to console and to sing."

Madame is horrified. "God forbid! They'll turn it into a drunken mess. And on top of that, their voices ... goodness."

At this precise moment, both of the Lollies make their entrance. Both are chattering incessantly, "Great that you invited us! We haven't been to a burial in a real long time. I guess we forgot the flowers, but we sure brought a lot of stuff to drink."

The second Lollie joins in, "I guess from now on, only silence will surround you."

An old man dodders over to them. "You two seem very familiar to me. Where do I know you from? Tell me (hic)! From another burial? You look so sad. Do I know you?"

The Lollies disappear quickly. Aunt Hilda has just arrived, and she turns to the lady of the house. "I have come here purely out of respect. From now on, the divine and—alas!—silenced voice will sing hymns and songs of praise in heavenly jubilation with all the other German angels."

The dodderer saves the lady the trouble of answering. "What? Silenced voices sing songs of praise? What a stupid thing to say. Cheers!"

Aunt Hilda is not to be derailed. "The great song of love never ends."

Instead of adulation, she receives only blank stares from her rather tipsy spectators, whereupon she grabs a glass from a servant carrying a tray through the room.

The great lady of the upper aristocracy pushes her way through the throngs and points with one black-gloved finger at a millefleurs tapestry hanging behind the singer lying in state. "There's one… and there (hic), and there (hic), and that one."

"Iss all Greek t'me," babbles an old party member well on his way to the Land of Drunk, as he tries to lift up the heavy cloth over the catafalque.

The general stops him and announces in an almost dying voice, "Dear mourners. My darling wife and I (hic) have decided to give our (hic) beloved brother in song over to the blessed water, just like the ancient Germanic tribes."

"Thass a good way t'cut costs," exclaims the rather forward old geezer.

The general tosses another one back (using a glittering swastika-decorated cut crystal shot glass of the finest caliber), pulls the black cloth from the catafalque, and reveals to the astounded, rather tipsy masses a high, beautiful, wooden… birdcage that has been placed on a billiards table. With a solemn—thanks to the many glasses—if rather erratic gesture, he removes a dead canary from the cage and kisses it on its silent beak.

Then he displays the bird to the flabbergasted, drunken mourners with these words: "A final farewell, my (hic) my dear, dead (hic) friend. Sing on in the skies above Germany!"

He walks solemnly, but a little uncertainly around the perimeter of the so-called catafalque while his wife, weeping uncontrollably, opens a side door in the hallway and beckons him there with a weakening hand gesture. "One last goodbye kiss, my (hic) dearest of all singers," he murmurs in a tear-choked voice, staggers behind the door to the heavy gong beats of an adjutant, who tries to make the Hitler salute but without success as he is holding two glasses in his outstretched hand instead of the gong. Then all of the mourners clearly hear the rush of the general's flushing toilet. A funny old lady, also in black, laughs irreverently and cries, "Good Lord, that's what he meant by the blessed water? No, seriously? Hahahahaha!" She can hardly hold herself upright over the force of her drunken laughter.

"They're cuckoo! What a couple of birdbrains!" says the merry old geezer, without doddering even once.

The mournful action was thus ended, and there was a party in this house devoid of birdsong that none of those present would soon forget. On the next day, however, hardly anyone could remember why he (or she) had come; they were all so soused.

---

First *Post Scriptum*:

After 1945, only a pile of rubble remained of this great, noble German house with its handsome gardens. The entire de-Nazified grounds became part of a neosocialist area crowned by a wall that was rather unhandsome. The death strip on the red side of the wall was simply unspeakable.

Of the general's family, only the good, loyal, German shepherd named Wotan miraculously survived. Later, in the '90s of the last inglorious century, the rest of the ghostliness disappeared along with the wall and made room for a wild green area. If you have good ears, you may be able to hear among the bushes and trees of reconquering Nature the soft, melodious twittering of a single, invisible bird—like a voice from another world...

Yes, oh yes, "Heaven and Earth must pass,... but music lives forever." Let's hope.

Second *Post Scriptum*:

This sad story has not been invented in any way, but rather empathized from a merrily damp story from my friend Auguste Wirsing (we're both from Wuppertal, oh horrors). If you can believe this story, have a drink on me.

---

(This absurd piece was also performed as a theatrical farce at the Source Theater in Washington, D.C.)

# The Nihilist
## or, the new acquisition

The largest museum of ultramodern art in the most art-hungry city in the nation recently received an anonymous donation of a gigantic painting by the "most significant artist of the modern era," Tom Foolrie. Critics reacted to the previews with fantastic reviews, indeed shouts of praise, like the following:

"A large, almost empty surface with one line—inspired! Art reduced to the singular! It resurrects the old myths, shines as bright as a resurgence of eternities, the eternal eternally captured! . . An unknown dialogue between the eternal and the momentary, sense and the senses, creativity ignited! The absolute last word, a painted cry for help on the verge of falling into the void within ourselves ... a grandiose lifeline."

In another place (from a puffed-up talking head from the *Frankfurter Post* with the title of "Doctor"):

"The complexity of great works such as this is often lost on the uneducated because they only see the surface. But what depth! The triumph of the simple line as a symbol reduced to its essence expands the immensity of the massive surface into the transcendental! ... Not a mere brushstroke, a stroke of genius! It is a witness to the spirituality of the single true genius, the momentum to move us away from the creative deficit of the masses and... gently... to move into an all-encompassing efficiency of identity... Here, intuition is the magic word. The work is pure magic. In plain English, this work is an existential impulse providing the initial spark of a completion of thought from the psychic realm, in a manner of speaking, a latent impetus from within... Quite

116

plausible, by the way, and not comparable to the paranormal executions of the often-unspeakable "new realists," who really only create platitudes and, one speculates, are merely attached to the unconfident, monotonous, and bombastic scenario of simply aping the old masters! Wonderful! Enlightening!"

If you speak and write in the press this clearly, then no one will ever dare to contradict you. However, there were far more profound critiques—appended at the end of this story—for those who may be interested, such as the art history student still reaching for words. Here, however, I can already promise that the reader's ears will prick up when these words are spoken aloud as desired by their author; she herself recited the little text in the ladies' restroom (according to an anonymous witness). This formidable, printed cacophony of words will appear even more amazing when one considers the fact that, as a less profound, or less sensitive visitor to the museum commented: "there's hardly anything to see on the picture at all."

Another voice could be heard in the museum (and was piously ignored by the enthusiastic critics): "What's up with this one line, this dash here along the bottom going back and forth between thick and thin? The whole rest of the canvas has been primed, but it's blank. Oh well, at least it's signed and framed."

You wouldn't think it was possible, but this short statement hits the nail on the head. Besides the line across the bottom, the newly acquired painting was empty. The highly-praised signature didn't add much either; it was hidden in the lower left-hand corner even farther down than the celebrated line.

"Wait just a minute!" called the museum director three days after the opening of the new gallery with the special exhibit. ["Art is art is art is…"] "Something isn't right here."

He called in several experts and even the artistic "prima donna" himself. "Is this gigantic painting here yours, Foolrie?" he asked.

The experts continued to stare at the work—or "void"—with total admiration, but to everyone's surprise, the master announced, "It could be mine, but it isn't."

"Why not, for God's sake?" groaned the museum director who, unfortunately, already knew the reason.

"Because I always sign in the lower *right* hand corner!"

That hit home. The experts' religious astonishment gave way to punitive ogling at the gigantic (once lovely) empty canvas. "It's, it's true," the chief expert (with two doctorates and a professorship) stammered out. His adoring attitude seemed to change a little.

"So, where is the original, Foolrie?" the beleaguered director ventured to ask. This painting here is ..."

Mr. Foolrie took the words right out of his mouth. "A copy obviously, but not by me. I can copy much better than that." To the horror of the expert committee, Foolrie added, "It's a pathetic copy, too. My line always starts out thin and, only at the end, because of my ingenious pressure on the brush, does it become wider, more tactile, more challenging." Embarrassed silence like that in a cathedral, or a courtroom before an impeding verdict, is pronounced throughout the room.

"Then all of the glowing reviews are crap," the director sighed. "They were lauding the genius on a... a copy. Unbelievable! What sort of tom foolery—sorry, Foolrie—who was the miscreant here? Out with it! It had to be someone in-house. Who was it?"

He sent the ladies and gentlemen from the expert committee out and remained behind with Tom Foolrie.

Mr. Foolrie, who really wasn't ashamed at all, tried to comfort his friend and benefactor, to whom he owed his breakthrough onto the international scene, in his own way. "Hey, it doesn't really matter who did this picture, Armin. I still have four or five of these large-size paintings in my studio, all of them nicely signed in the lower right-hand corner, even before, as the press so charmingly puts it, I created the stroke of genius or the enigmatical line."

The director turned quite pale indeed. "Are you out of your mind? The whole world has known since the private viewing that this is a unique work. One of one! Copies? Replicas? Duplicates? Not in my museum! Leave me alone before I have a heart attack. I have to figure out how we can avoid a scandal. Get out of here! Now!" The foolish Mr. Foolrie skulked out, but hid himself behind the exit door and was forced to, able to, permitted to hear the following scene.

The director, Dr. A., called his assistant who, after a quick whispered conference, called the head conservationist who in turn called his chief restorer. The restorer seemed to have an idea and, in a few minutes, Alois, who was in charge of the cleaning ladies and generally known as the Factotum, was brought forth. Mr. Foolrie couldn't believe his ears when he heard Alois admit that on the very first day, a week before the private viewings, he had unfortunately "sort of" damaged the gigantic canvas while pushing it into a storage room—just a few little scratches though. A new object, one of the other acquisitions by Heini or someone like that, a metallic montage, was standing in the way and ripped small tears in the canvas, very fine tears, more like scratches. Alone with no witnesses around, he decided to correct the situation. He just wanted to help. Alois found a very large, empty canvas that had served as staff in the previous exhibit, took a good long look at the damage, and got to work. He saw that there was just this line going along the bottom, in brownish red, the favorite color of the oh-so-damaged artist, and made up a good color mixture that was similar to the original and, painted the line on the new canvas from left to right and then signed the painting quickly too, unfortunately in the lower left-hand corner instead of in the lower right-hand corner. He heard footsteps and had to quickly hide what he was doing. Alois was convinced that the signature was just as simplistic as the long line and all he wanted to do was to save the honor of the museum and the private viewings, and the honor of the master. The footsteps came closer and Erna Bosomjoy (who had already achieved worldwide fame with her involvement in an incident concerning a bathtub) helped him to cut up the damaged original and to fit the new painting, *his* work (he actually said that—"*my* work," in tones that carried a deep conviction) into the available frame. So there were two people to help the museum in its time of need. They only made a few slight changes to the frame.

The swindled museum director turned red with rage. "Cutting up, painting, a few slight changes—what next? You're fired Alois. Save us, indeed! You have disgraced me, the museum, Mr. Foolrie, and German art to the highest degree possible."

"And even the press," the cleaning lady, Erna, interjected. "We went to so much effort with them, sir."

Her boss was going from red to pink, to a pale so white that he looked like Snow White's brother and snarled at both of them. "The press must know nothing of this! Zero! Zip! Understood?"

"Yes, of course, otherwise it would be an absolute scandal—for them, too. Those idiots didn't even look hard enough to notice that the signature was on the wrong side. Alois, your mistake," was the almost amused, insulting reply from poor, snarled-at Erna.

Alois was even bold enough to ask, "Considering *those* circumstances, can I stay?"

Completely stunned, his boss replied, "Yes, of course, Alois, you can stay, but hold your tongue. Not even any deathbed confessions of this to anyone. Do I have your word?"

Alois was in complete agreement, but couldn't keep himself from suggesting: "It would be really easy for me to just paint another canvas with the signature in the lower right-hand corner."

That was the last straw for the director, who shattered his reputation for being level-headed and conciliatory by shouting: "Get out!"

Alois and Erna had hardly disappeared into the basement by way of the elevator when the master behind the door took heart. He went over to his museum crony and lamented, "It's enough to make you cry, Armin. There's no more respect for the great men of art, not for you, not for me. But I know a way out of our mess."

"So you were listening, you fool?" he asked, answering his own question. "Talk to me! You can see for yourself how immense the damage is—how do you plan to avert it?"

Without batting an eye, the great artist said, "As I told you, I still have a few more originals in my studio."

"Now I'm really getting sick of this. Do I need to preach you a sermon about unique, copies, and replicas or something?"

An ominous pause followed. Tom wanted to distract him from that train of thought. "Lucky for us that Alois didn't sign along one of the sides or up top, you know, like that thing, you know the guy I mean, Bawitz or some other witz. I can't even remember his first name."

"George. You always call him 'the guy with the gag.'"

"Right, that's him. The one who puts his oilskin on their heads—it works—but he's not a genius like Pollock, and then signs them. What a gag, seriously. People fell for it left and right. All we need now is someone who paints his pictures right through the canvas without priming it and then demands that the back be seen as the front, heh-heh-heh."

"There's a guy like that already in Arizona."

The local genius: "Armin, that shows that you have an eye for quality, that you don't let any paintings in your museum, our museum, that are signed the wrong way, even though the stuff is being shown everywhere, even in national galleries. What a simple gag—put on its head and nothing else. It makes me laugh."

Then the highly praised artist, who coincidentally did not originate the white wall looming before him and (according to the press) whose "overemphasized lack of content lends even greater eloquence to the fascination of the silent emptiness of the work," the celebrated master, attempts a tortured smile for his fellow painter.

"Drop the joking, Foolrie, think about how you can preserve your own reputation. I just had a thought. How about you become even more consistent and just don't paint anything on your famous canvases anymore? Not one line, not one stroke, no signature, the emptiness could be your trademark, the antithesis of the horror *vacui*. That's it! You will be celebrated because of your daring lack of painting, you will be numbered among the great nihilists. Especially by your little friend at the *Post*. She always sees more than is on the surface of a painting."

Friend Foolrie awakens from his much-discussed profundity and sensitivity and responds almost exultantly, "Wow! Armin thanks for the great idea. Apply for the copyright straight away! I'll go get to work immediately."

The director is completely taken aback. "Get to work? What work?"

Our Foolrie replies, "Framing empty canvases, of course. Bravo, Armin!"

He hurries out without hearing the murmured comments of his muse: "He falls for every joke. Well, that's why he's called Foolrie." The director then returns to the hallowed halls of his art institution.

In spite of the concrete walls, which are about a yard thick, booming laughter can be heard coming from the basement. Who is laughing at whom?

All the museums today are full to the brim with these pictures of complete emptiness, or rather empty completeness, which were painted—pardon me, artistically framed—at that time, because everywhere great value is placed on being up with the latest trend, whatever the cost. And the artist as nihilist? Cashing in with incredible amounts of money and laughing all the while, he says in private, "What's next? I'm ready."

However you choose to turn it, or shift it, this story is (turned on its side) at an end.

---

## The famous Postscript

Dear reader, I am sure you, for your part, are thinking of the actual, complete emptiness in the museums of the ultramodern: only the air, the breath of the invisible visual (or vice versa) fills the high rooms, the thinkers' brains of the initiators, the gawking masses of visitors who are for once able to gaze into emptiness (and pay admission for it, too!) and the celebrated, absolute nothing will even help to cut costs. No reproductions, no need to print now-superfluous catalogs, no placards, empty though they may be, pure nothingness, into which the night watchman of the Bonaventura gazed: nothing everywhere, Nothingness, nothing at all. How futile the little person appears before this great emptiness that, I repeat, looks like nothing, oh so small. And then a child asks, "Daddy, could we maybe go to a museum where there's something to see?" But his father, the former museum director, who had the splendid, money-saving idea, stares silently into... nothing.

Below is a selection of reviews of the (alas, copied) work of Tom Foolrie from the morning after the private viewing, when the thing was still considered a unique work. These are the most German statements from the competent authorities on the genius that is satisfied with the achievement of a single line but then with even less... Naturally, these sentences are spoken in the play, but are overheard by Alois and Erna and annotated by their hilarious retorts. These quotes are from my play *The New Acquisition*, which continues to wait and wait for its premiere...

"The perplexity and central prerogative in the aspects of the master (Tom Foolrie) are already illuminated by his exquisite sketches (from ten lines down to one, boldly vibrating), a true simulacrum in which the most eloquent critiques associate and which, in the future, shall challenge even greater spirits." "The poor, pitiful human eye is not sufficient to asses, appreciate, and *nolens volens* evaluate the enigmatical in his artistic achievement...." "This gigantic image is a lonely zenith in German contemporary art, which is on its way to a return to associative-imagistic abstraction thought in the totality..." "The linearity of this pregnant brushstroke as the primary content and true statement of the completed work is minimalistic genius, creating a completely new equilibrium for the senses." "The insanity of everyday symbolized by a single line—how daring!" (The reply from eavesdropping Erna: "Art is on the line here!") "Here, the artistic gesture of a truly great artist combines by means of a brown-red trace of symbiosis with the Vita of the universal [sic!], vibrates once again, and, at the end, as the stroke of the brush shows... breathes... out." "This mystical line usurps all conventional figurative associations, because here, virtually for the first time, an idea has been transubstantiated into a work of art without the detour of form: a pure sanctification!" (Alois: "Any idiot can draw a line like that!") "This starting point and ending point releases aspirations for futuristic execution of German art... The mere imagistic is confidently overcome... His nature of the modern libertine banishes the heaviness of our globe into the pure whiteness of his splendid canvas... the proverbial red lines of vital excessivity have never been captured as dominantly as here and it is reminiscent of ancient studies of the Golden Section, without it even being used here... Here, the form is brought to the smallest conceivable nominator—because art lies in the leaving out!" ("Someday he'll leave the line out, too," says Erna.)

"A blatantly remarkable miracle! The illuminated commemoration of orthogonal elements that summarizes in the vacuum of the totality of the surface new thoughts of dislocation and translocation and subtly observes other potential causalities...." (Erna: "You can put it that way too....") "This joyously hurled line, this meaning-rich lifeline, in the bright fog of primordial white combines all disparate elements into a new, fascinating homogeneity, simultaneously hermetic and an enigma: It can be said that Tom Foolrie is a joyous destroyer of assurance!" ("It's like a scratch and dent sale!" cries Alois.) "Hidden here is a complete palate of stupendous excursions, no longer bound by image, that crystallizes all of the irritating configurations into a contrast-filled work in the most ingenious [sic!] manner possible..." "So it may be postulated as follows: a modern artist does not explain either himself nor his work, he allows them to be explained by others! Where else would the German art world find the enormous (ham-fisted?) statement on the cryptical, eclectic dimensions of new utopias?" (Alois: "Then the listener and reader turn with horror and think: what a load of crap!")

# The Minuet

Johann Sebastian Bach died 250 years ago today, February 15, 2000. Appropriately enough, the classical music station here is celebrating the occasion. Joyously, I listen to the last movement of Brandenburg Concerto, number 1, the Minuet, among others. My legs twitch, I begin to hop, to dance, to whirl all through the kitchen, almost keeping time with the music. I am made young again by Bach's music. But alas, I have to interrupt my frolicking when I glance at the clock; it's time to run to the kindergarten bus stop and pick up little Robert. Once I am in the house again, Bach's heavenly tones are muted, for I have to make lunch for the little one (canned noodles are the quickest) and comfort him since he has misbehaved again and earned himself a seat on the bus separated from the other children. Now he has even begun to blubber. When I ask him about his schoolwork, though, he perks right up, and shows me his painted letters, lovely and bright and almost legible. He grows quiet for a moment when he finds crayons behind the cat food. I give him paper and he gives me a few minutes of peace and reflection. I breathe a sigh of relief. The cats sleep.

Then I am reminded of a time from my youth, when I was still the hey-here-I-come kind of guy, and was a sought-after dancer and danced the minuet. It was about 1957, in the city of the monorail. I was being trained at the Vorwerk carpet company as an industrial textile designer for machine-woven carpets, a patroneur, and the last person in Germany to have that job title. All eight apprentices, four girls and four boys from the drawing studio, were called upon one day for whatever long-forgotten reason to study a dance to be performed in period costumes in order to make a good impression at an upcoming party given by the weaving company. We practiced, we danced, two times two pairs, to all kinds of practice music. We rented baroque-era costumes and looked wonderfully old-fashioned. The studio head decided that our music could only be a minuet by Boccherini: "Short and cheerful and easy to dance to." His idea was perfect, our efforts rather less so. Especially the oversteps, bending the right knee and crossing the left leg over it, similar to a glissade, changing step quickly, made us flounder especially badly: become unsure, grab the wrong partner, fall out of rhythm, cross our legs the wrong way. We tangled ourselves up even to the point of slips and falls. We would have almost preferred to pass up the pleasure of dancing, in spite of the wonderful music.

So, I decided the next time I visited my Aunt Emmi; I would try out the dance there with my cousin. She danced well and with abandon, and soon we practiced the minuet together. The crown jewel of my aunt's apartment was a gigantic aquarium filled with dozens of exotic fish along with real and fake corals. It stood precisely in the middle of a medallion on her largest Persian rug. We danced carefully around it. As our dancing became more and more boisterous—without music, we accompanied ourselves by humming the melody—I thought I could easily bring a lift into our hopping about, the so-called choreography, because Ilonka was as light as a puppet back then. We turned, daintily crossed our legs, and performed a rococo-style bow. I whirled her high into the air, she laughed; I threw her upwards again, caught her again—it was working wonderfully. My cousin and I—what a pair! All at once, the Persian rug slid along the floor and I slipped, staggered, lost my balance with Ilonka in my arms. She lost her balance, too, and we fell, arms around each other, into the side of my absent aunt's aquarium. It shattered and water rushed like a flood over the floor of the entire apartment. The fish splashed down as well, of course, and the poor fish that landed in dry spots soon flopped their last flop. Soaked to the skin but somehow uninjured in spite of the thousands of glass slivers, Ilonka managed to pick herself up while I still fumbled around on the floor. We started off by collecting the fish that were still flopping around; then, we filled up the bathtub and threw them in, always sliding along the floor. Walking was out of the question until we were sure all of the fish that were still alive had been saved. The dead ones we quickly flushed down the toilet, Aunt Emmi could splash back in at any time.

Apparently, she was running late today and we had time to encircle and sop up the water with mops, brooms, cloths, and sponges, and then pick up the pieces of glass. Naturally, all of the oriental rugs, high-quality machine-made carpets from Vorwerk, were soaked through. We rolled them up and did our best to squeeze the water out of them outside the front door. A few more flopping fish fell out.

The worst was over by the time Aunt Emmi arrived and gave us both a dressing down. For days after the dancing accident, or the "water minuet," my aunt claimed it smelled terrible and she swept at least a handful of dead fish out from under the furniture. As a punishment, I was not invited to her house for six months to play garbage disposal, in other words, to eat her leftovers. Back then, I had an insatiable appetite.

But now, the minuet was on the program as the company party began. As we dutifully, daintily, and demurely turned our minuet circles, I saw Ilonka out in the audience. Suddenly, I was flooded by the memory of the aquarium disaster. This signal from my brain activated my laughter reflex. How awful! I began laughing, first quietly to myself, and then it burst loose. My beautifully costumed dance partner forgot the crossover step. She stepped on my foot, I stepped on hers, we stumbled and I was shaking with laughter. I couldn't hear the Boccherini anymore. We were ungently shoved aside by the other dancing couple, with whom we were supposed to be dancing a four-person pirouette. I shoved back, we lost all balance and fell crosswise one over the other—all eight of us—onto the hard floor of the temporary wooden stage.

That was it for our little dance. The audience clapped and cheered with enthusiasm because the festively assembled employees of Vorwerk all assumed that this abrupt end of the minuet had been just as tumultuously studied and rehearsed as the rest of the dance. I have never again had such a resounding success on any other stage—but *behind* a stage ... I'll tell you about that later.

# Il Ballo Dell'Ingrate

**W**hat Tommy doesn't learn, Tom will never understand. This age-old morsel of German folk wisdom has apparently lost its educational significance in our day and age. Today, it seems as though no one has any desire to learn anything or to gain an education for higher purposes; no, there must always be an instant reward or payment (without it having been earned). There is no question of "What can I do?" only "What's in it for me?" Even the old saying, "Rome wasn't built in a day," seems meaningless.

Back when I was still a Tommy (long before I had matured into tomfoolery, to give my less intelligent readers something to laugh at), I decided of my own free will to learn everything I could that would be helpful to my talent. In the course of my apprenticeship years, I benefited from contact with the following career paths: designer and patroneur (pattern drawings for textiles), card puncher (for jacquard looms), art student (academic), a puller of strings, a real manipulator (I really did spend my semester breaks working in a factory producing strings), engraver (for silk printing), prop manager (for stage and film), carpet knotter, commercial artist, weaver (Aubusson), cartoonist (for tapestries), some others as well, and stage design assistant. It is from this esoteric career that this story arises.

An amusing beginning can often lead to a painful end. After several forays into southern Germany, which were very helpful to me as short educational trips, I returned to Wuppertal after 1960 and found employment—temporary, as always—at the opera as a scenery painter and assistant to a wise, experienced scenery designer, who had provided multiple theaters with unusual, well thought through decorations that were always based on the music or the text. Heiner Wendel's set designs were considered great works of art and were admired as such— rightfully so. With particular dedication, I helped at first with the painting of minute models and then enlarging the models to two-dimensional panoramas that serve as the only background in many pieces, especially in ballet. Our team was famous for making paintings so natural the players on stage would move back a few steps so as to not bump into a column, staircase, or wall, even though such obstacles were not three-dimensional at all, but rather were painted on a completely flat canvas. The optical illusion was perfect. Naturally, the audience fell for our subterfuge as well and believed they were looking at completely furnished rooms where there was really only a painted cloth. Irritating perhaps, but that was our contribution to the magic of the stage.

One fine day, when we were working on scenery for Monteverdi's ballet *"Il Ballo dell'Ingrate,"* ("The Ball of the Ingrates")—panoramic sky with white clouds on a white background that, with the right lighting, turned into storm clouds and a threatening night sky—I was given the task of designing and painting offset pieces: benches, tables, walls, towers, and a portico. However, it had to be done in a great hurry, the premiere loomed less than a week away. (The first scenery concept had been trashed and now we were supposed to have a lot more onstage.) Luckily, although I was a mere assistant myself, I had an assistant of my own who was the younger brother of a famous composer and could paint as industriously as I could without hesitating or babbling about questions of detail. The orders from on high were to immediately drop everything else and to start on the large painting surfaces in accordance with the current plan of the chief scenery designer. One set of instructions for mixing paint read, "Mix one pot of light blue into each of five buckets of white paint, pour into the paint vat and mix well with three buckets of glue and one bucket of lime." I thoughtlessly delegated this base job to my assistant Jürgen. I was sure he could manage simple stirring, although he wasn't always on top of things. I knew that he liked to daydream and, after playing on his spinet, would sometimes seem to be not entirely there mentally; his wife Xenia seemed to be this way as well. But he performed his work conscientiously, undisturbed by mental absence. Therefore, especially in light of the short time we had to finish, I saw no reason to check every vat of paint to make sure the mixtures were all correct. I had both of my hands full and I painted the walls of reinforced canvas set up in the painting room with the paint that Jürgen handed me. I had to work through an entire night as well (I wasn't in a union) and, on the morning of the dress rehearsal, I fell into a deep sleep on a mattress behind the stage so that I would be awake for the premiere that evening. I was awakened at 6:00 in the evening. The curtain was supposed to rise on the premiere performance at 8:00.

How excited we all were. Such disorder in front of, on, and behind the stage was hardly rare, but seldom as hectic, with such questioning glances, lost-looking dancers, and coarse stagehands. In order to escape the tumult, I suggested to Jürgen that we should climb up to the lighting catwalk high above the stage and watch the great event from behind the curtain.

In passing, I asked him whether anything had gone wrong at the dress rehearsal, because only then will the premiere be a success. He grinned back, "Everything—and I mean absolutely everything—went wrong. It was great."

Good enough reason to be excited about the premiere, but I wanted specifics. "What went wrong, for example?"

"Oh, nothing special. I just told the jumpers they shouldn't lean on our painted walls, even if they do look like real walls."

"And?"

"Well, they were keeping their distance anyway because there was always this crackling and snapping sound coming from the walls as soon as the lights were on them. But that was all."

"What crackling and snapping in the backdrops? You mixed the paint correctly, didn't you?"

In his thoughts, he was playing the spinet again. "Yes, just like you wrote: one bucket of glue and three buckets of lime into each paint vat. That bone glue stinks like hell, by the way."

He was slow to catch my horror, until I had to say, "The other way around, for heaven's sake! You idiot! Do you know what it means if you mix in too much lime instead of glue? The backdrops tense up—they could snap."

"Snap?"

"Yes, burst! A few minutes of light on them are enough—the lime dries out, bursts off, and smacks everyone on stage on the head. What kind of tension do you think there is in a canvas that is too dry? It will rip. On the other hand, more glue than lime, yes, that will be a catastrophe."

"So what?"

(My prophecies were about to be fulfilled in a terrible—but comically grotesque—manner.) I stared at him.

"Are you out of your mind? What do you mean, so what? Sit down, but keep a bucket of water ready with a hose."

He obeyed, in his dreamy, foolish way. Then we sat down and waited, spellbound, for the inevitable. Monteverdi's beautiful music began, as though coming from another world. I looked in the dark corner of the catwalk and saw the mis-mixer cowering on the boards, without even a stool. His hands were folded, as if in prayer. He could use some, I thought.

The overture was over; the dancing began with wonderful audacious steps, with bows, with elegant gestures and breathtaking leaps by the danseurs, with graceful arabesques and gravity-defying pirouettes by the ballerinas. It was enchanting. Applause for each scene swelled up and ebbed. This continued until the music became more peaceful, more lost in reverie, to create tension before the necessary opening of the gates of Hell. Something else was creating tension as well. First, there was a soft creaking and then a louder crackling. The dancers seemed confused, lost their orientation to the audience, and looked more and more towards the set decoration, toward our blue and white painted canvases. I foresaw something terrible, because the lighting would certainly now bring forth a shining, glistening, hot beam. Plainly speaking, the too small amount of glue threatened to dry out under the lights' heat and the excessive amount of lime would quickly dry out until it would tense the canvas to the point of tearing. Some first, fine cracks appeared. (If I were a Catholic, I would have to call on the appropriate saint to show his world-entrancing holiness with silence and absence.) Just then, some dancing Ephesians, clad entirely in white, pushed the eternally long benches and tables into the center of the stage on silent wheels, so that all of the performers could take part in a joyous feast once more before the upcoming journey into Hell, only moments before the damnation was already being implied in the music.

As the musical climax swelled forth, instead of the magical opening of the stage and change into the underworld, there came an earsplitting crack, which can be found neither in the choreography, nor in Monteverdi's score. Then a second and a third followed, until an explosion of bursting backdrops removed the rest. The poor dancers! They ran, leapt, and climbed for their lives as scraps of the hard, hot textile walls flew in all directions. Then the frames broke, splintered, shot all around.

The music played on in glorious overloud tones, as written, but there was no dancing to be seen; rather, a chaotic ruckus in sputtering light on a self-destructing stage with a grotesque ballet that no choreographer could invent. All hell had broken loose. It was the result of the work of an unlearned, rather uneducated, assistant.

I thought I could hear clapping over the tumult. It escalated to such storms of applause as the Wuppertal opera has never heard before, or since. The audience, inexperienced in Monteverdi's work, was raving with excitement. The audience was quite thoroughly convinced that they were watching the best choreographed staged chaos by a genius director with unparalleled surprise effects. Even the confused, turbulent flight of the dancers from the bright stage to the inviting darkness of the side curtains seemed genuinely chaotic. Now laughter could be heard above the clamoring bustle—shrill, screeching, and very close to me. It came from Jürgen, who was doubled up with laughter and was causing the catwalk to bend and vibrate.

"There, there!" he cried, pointing to the unlucky, terrified danseurs and their poor partners, all of whom were trying to save themselves from the offset pieces exploding all around them, dancing a chaotic choreography as could only be imagined in Hell itself.

All that was missing was fire. Instead, there was rain onstage because Jürgen made the catwalk shake to the point that the water bucket emptied itself bit by bit, which looked to the spectators like rain ordered by the director. The music broke off when it occurred to the musicians that something wasn't quite right up there. Slowly, laughter began to well up in me, I chortled first, looked at Jürgen, and buried my horror under laughter. The audience itself prolonged the shortened ballet performance—it demanded curtain call after curtain call and couldn't get enough of the astonishing behavior of the dancers, who somehow managed to come forward for bows in spite of pretended injuries.

Even the reviewer in the next morning's paper spoke of an "incredible success of the director and performers, who spectacularly overcame a small stage accident, which caused the performance to be broken off. They turned this accident into not only the best that this stage has ever seen, but to exalt it into a grandiose spectacle of myth, a visually complete chaos of vital individuality. Artistic creativity knows no bounds when it unleashes itself."

The reviewer did not, however, mention the 13 injuries, the enormous damage to the stage decoration, the cause of the whole incident, or the simple fact that this remained the only performance of *Il Ballo* in Wuppertal. And why should he?

My conclusion? Truth is still far better than fiction.

# The Last Conversation
## *in memoriam*
## Gertrud Dahlmann-Stolzenbach

The winter of 1988 had come early; nature had gone to sleep. My steps were heavy on my way to St. Augustine's Home in Munich, as if a dark premonition impeded my movement. We didn't take the elevator to the second floor; I like to carry the stroller up a few flights of stairs. We entered her room and exchanged greetings. First, I introduced her to David, the Army captain from Stuttgart, and then, to her great delight, to little Micah (in German, Micha). He is nine months old and curious, contentedly crawling around on her bed. She wants to know everything about the child and cannot believe it when I tell her that there are a lot of things I can't do anymore because of the child, such as going to the theater, to concerts, or to the movies. When I tell her I haven't seen a movie for five months, she looks at me with wide eyes.

"Really? Not one? Not a single one?" she asks. As she speaks, her partially paralyzed left hand is playing with Micah's little hand. I am so reluctant to begrudge her this joy over playing with the little boy that I keep quiet: Yes, I have seen a movie recently, one of those where the Americans try to deal with their past in Vietnam, but that falls flat as a film as well…. We laugh at Micah's contortions as he chases after her silver wristwatch.

"And theater? No opera anymore either? And you love it so much … with Gabi, such a cheerful person." She wants to know.

"No, I miss out on those pleasures as well. Out of responsibility for the child." She looks at me and acts surprised.

"You don't say! You say that so matter-of-factly. I would have never expected to see even a trace of that in you."

"Of what?" I play dumb. I like to hear the answer.

"Well, that you would ever take responsibility for anything or anyone ... I just can't believe it. But the child is right here, on my stomach, and I have to believe you. I'm glad to believe you, dear. Hey, guess who was lying on me yesterday!"

"On your stomach?"

"Where else?"

"Gertrud!"

"It was Thomas Mann! There he is, over there. The thick book. The entire, wonderful Joseph legend!"

The little boy laughs along with us out of pure joy. I secretly place a chocolate Santa wrapped in colored foil in her hand. She can't feel it, but she notices it and strokes it like a child. This joyous spirit, I think to myself, what a terrible contrast to her physical condition. It scared me to death when we came into her room. Her response? "Go back out!" she called to me. "I haven't done my hair yet today. I haven't even combed it! Out with you!" Oh, Gertrud, I thought, how vain you still are at your age.

"What are you thinking?"

"You're still the same old Gertrud," I ventured to say. The way she's combing her hair is funny; it's not making her hair any prettier. I put a second chocolate Santa on the white sheet.

"How come? What do you mean? Me, old? ... Have you got any more of those?"

Of course. I put a third Santa on her bed. "You always see right through me when I'm thinking of you. I was wondering why you have to be primped just to receive an old friend?"

"That's how it ought to be." Period.

But because I myself am so fond of her wild, wavy, snow-white hair, the way it shifts with her every movement, I ask David to take a picture of her with the little one in her arms. David is an unwilling participant in this visit, since he knows her only from hearsay. A clamor erupts; she doesn't want to do it uncombed. That's what she gets for letting us in, even though we could have waited outside for a few minutes. Simply put: ready for the stage—like so many previous encounters with her—with GDS. Her name was too long for us, so Gabi and I started just referring to her as GDS. Have you been to see GDS? How is GDS doing? What a woman! Only once in your lifetime do you meet a woman like that. I manage to distract her briefly with the fourth Santa. The picture is taken and, because she is still bristling theatrically, quickly another one and another one. With dismay, I notice how Micah has pushed aside the sheet as he played on the bed, exposing an almost translucent leg, a leg that can hardly be called alive anymore. This is the end! Her entire life force is concentrated in her head; the rest of her body has already begun its journey. The body is only a shell for the soul; the naked truth of it lies before me. Her leg is in the middle of dying. And her spirit? So bright and soulful, so vital and yearning for joy and dialogue that I suddenly feel quite wretched. I look into her eyes and cannot find even the slightest trace of … death. But she is lying here dying, I tell myself. Her body is visibly deteriorating. Will I be able to see Gertrud again? A quiet, sad foreboding arises. Little Micah laughs and fidgets. The shadow of something large wanders through the room. All of a sudden, the winter sun comes out and shines right into the room. The metal rod above the bed throws a wandering shadow, so that it looks like a gallows. On the shadow gallows hangs … a Santa. A smile flits across her sunken face, which looks changed to me in the transition from bright light to shadow.

"There, take a look! A gallows for your humor. And who's hanging on it? Look! In reality, it's me and not Santa." What is she trying to say? To speak of death within the aura of such shining vitality surrounding her would be utterly absurd.

"You usually have so many silly questions for me. What's up with you? No more interest in an old woman, eh? We're friends; there's no taboo between us. So come on, speak up! Something's bothering you. Tell me."

Might this be our last conversation? Am I speechless because I suspect it? Well, okay …

"Could you do me a favor and try speaking part of Hannelore Schroth's monologue into the tape recorder again? Can you do that still?"

"Typical. That's so brash of you, to ask me if! That's ridiculous—of course I can! Which part? You're thinking that I'll soon be watching the flowers grow from below, aren't you? But it's still winter, just wait. Miss Schroth and her early death, heaven knows what that's good for; everything has its purpose. You were lucky enough to have her motherly help on your plays. You and mothers, I swear! But what am I talking about? You are my joy and then the child as well! How did you wind up with this roly-poly little guy? The same way as the Virgin Mary maybe?"

What should I say to that? I tell her the whole series of events, the mother's unwillingness to raise the child and other details that aren't just anybody's business. I stepped in as a replacement for a mother.

"Right, that's what I want to know, who's the mother. A blind person can see who the father is!" She looks at us. David and I grin over our bet, which doesn't confuse her at all. She nods.

"So what are you teaching the little one?"

I think about it briefly, and then admit with some emotion, "Gertrud, it seems to me as though I learned all of the songs of my youth only so that I could sing them to this child."

"Typical, Holger, you sing him something when language fails you. He should learn good German, the language of poets!"

"I sing because I'm happy." That's not how it's perceived.

"Do me a favor and don't sing here." She lovingly strokes the child's hair, and I see a blessing in her gesture. She looks wonderfully angelic, transcendental. We say goodbye with a heartfelt hug.

"It's not about our happiness; it's about hers," Heimtrud Vareschi, the other close friend I call after Traudi to warn of the approaching end, will say in a few hours. And she will add:

"Her soul is already living in the other world. She is not imagining when she talks about new recordings or lectures she gives before hundreds of imaginary listeners. She really does hear the applause! Her body has paid its debt, the soul has separated from it, and we can only be thankful witnesses to such strength of soul. She's one of a kind! It's good that you brought the baby by; that will cheer her up. It will distract her from the daily routine that you find even in a good home like St. Augustine's. We can be happy that she's doing as well as she is, under the circumstances."

And today, because deep snow is lying on GDS's grave, I am infinitely grateful to have had this last conversation with my dear friend and, with the same gratitude for the understanding of her other friends, I will share it and pass it on . On the day of the burial, when I will be far away, I will call Anna Lange, my other motherly friend, and ask her to lay a bouquet of deep red-blue flowers on the coffin, the colors of her silk dress when she still spoke to us, like a sybillic apparition, of the great German poets at the Lyceum Club on Maximilianstrasse in Munich.

Naturally, she had long since forgiven me for the time when, just because it was Carnival, right in the middle of her Schiller lecture, I cried "Helau!" and threw flowers onto her podium. That's how she saw it, but she had to interrupt the lecture and had great difficulty stifling her laughter. Back then no one thought of the possibility of ever having a last conversation.

"You'll never see her again," said David, who is more knowledgeable as a caregiver for the dying, after the very last farewell waves to the sound of a child's laughter. He was right. From now on, her face, almost transcendentally shining for joy, is only a memory.

A week after the burial, snowdrops sprout out of the dark mound of earth that covers her. Is that a symbol? Everyone is carried through life by his ability to create and perceive meaning. But may she rest in peace.

And, in thoughts, perhaps, Thomas Mann is lying on her again: "That one over there, the thick book …"

# Those Mouthy Berliners

I swear by all the fallen saints, this is what happened to me on my latest trip to Berlin in June 2001. This city, constantly torn down and built up, forever in flux, was more exhilarating to me than ever before. First, I wound up in the wrong S-Bahn trying to get to Wannensee (or was it Wannsee?) and then I got lost in the forest once I finally got to the right stop, namely Nikolaussee (or was it Nikolaisee?). When you're a tourist, you don't care about the endings of names as long as the beginning sounds right. A week later, I wanted to go splash around in the deep green lake with my kids. In brief, the following is my encounter with the proverbial Mouthy Berliners.

There was no end in sight to the shadowy, cool forest path from the S-Bahn station to the lake, so I asked a boy I passed whistling a Marlene Dietrich song (*"Das machen nur die Beine von Marlene"*) as he strolled down the path: "How much longer to the swimming area at the lake?"

"Three or four minutes," he replied, staring at me. Then he took a closer look, noticing my gray hair, and added, "ten for you." I was glad I could laugh at such a snappy remark.

Having finally arrived at the entrance to the swimming area, I look at the prices and mention, "I'm 61, by the way. Do you want to see my ID?"

The young, pretty cashier replied pertly, "So that's four Marks instead of six. Go on in, Gramps."

My laughter faded away, but a few minutes later on the beach I had a laughing fit and went swimming. First up to my feet, then up to my calves, then, shivering, up to my chest, I continued to wade further into the awfully cold water. The lifeguard read me the water temperature from a chalkboard on his chair: "Fifty degrees! Comfy, isn't it?"

Stout-heartedly, I dived under and imagined myself to be the only adventurous one there, a wet hero. But the noise of children behind me reconstructed my relationship to reality, which didn't seem quite so ice-cold anymore.

Two boys and a girl, all about ten years young, paddled by in a raft, called out to the lifeguard to turn on the water slide. They sprang into the water without first acclimating themselves and climbed the stairs to the water slide, which even from a distance looked very tall indeed, in front of me. I followed them. A large double curve was sufficient to accelerate the sliders, and we flew one after the other into the lake several meters from the slide. What a rush!

The girl had the temerity to ask, "Do you still get anything out of this at your age?"

At least she didn't call me Gramps, but language failed me and I swam away, back to the sunny, but cold beach. I wondered if her insolent question could be taken as a childish compliment. After all, the few other grownups were sitting on their beach chairs, basking in the weak sunlight, and didn't even dare to stick their big toe in the water. Naturally, the brats laughed at me, swimming after me as I let my imagination run loose.

"Down there in the lake, where I was diving, there are fish as large as small whales."

Braggart! If I had only kept my mouth shut.

"I bet you're one of those prehistoric whales, huh?"

And: "He's going in the water so he can see how cold it is in the graveyard."

One more verbal slap like that and I'm leaving. No, I'm leaving anyway.

"It's better to hear the truth from others than to lie to yourself," Martin Fritsch, director of the impressive Käthe Kollwitz Museum, commented a while later. He was glad I was able to laugh at it, too.

Yes, there's nowhere in the world you can laugh better than in Berlin.

# NEW LEGENDS
# OF THE RHINE

# The Watch on the Rhine

I am the Emperor. No jumped-up, dumb German nobody will ever blackmail me, Napoleon thought to himself in the olden days, but he thought it a trifle too loud. The giant brothers "Fasolt and Fafner" (see Wagner's opera, *Das Rheingold*) could read anybody's minds, even French ones. They were squatting atop the tower of the Rhineland-Palatinate palace, built on a rock in the very middle of the rushing river Rhine (i.e., near Koblenz). They kept a watchful eye on any foreigner, including any passing *empereur* trying to cross the river's ford without paying a toll; in short, all they wanted was blackmail.

The two big-muscled, small-brained giants were somehow unaware of a dragon-like monster sitting on the top cliffs of the next mountain much higher than they were. This monster was eager for any German-French encounter, as well. Spitting enormous flames of black (!) fire out of his hell of a mouth, he jumped down and swallowed the giants and almost caught the impudent Bonaparte conqueror as well, but he had managed to escape in a lamentable hurry eastwards towards Moscow.

The fleeing little emperor's French army got very cold feet in the river's waves and took to their heels after quickly engaging in the seductive love and the sweet embrace of some golden-haired Rhine maidens. There were exactly 4711 of the wet beauties, enough to have all their descendants baptized up to these days with the famed "Eau de Cologne," and to report this pretty story to us.

Of the two giant brothers nothing much remained but a spat-out, broken framework of bones, fleshless, bloodless, yet rock-hard. From this unusual material, those who outlived both the monster, the emperor and the Rhine-crossing hordes, have erected an awkward German memorial to remind us all of that unsuccessful crossing of the river. In later times a lot of "heroic" songs, such as "steadfast, proud and strong stands the German Watch on the Rhine," and other fantastic and rather

147

lunatic chorals were created, but mostly sang at merry carnival processions. This sounds like a delusion of utter foolishness, doesn't it?

For today, not a single German fairy-tale giant or jolly garden gnome is standing at that ford to guard the Rhine. See, how wrongly and how twisted Rhenish history can end.

# The Spiteful Sisters

This is just a little legend from the old days that has been revived; it's not some sort of "Tale from the Mists of Time." As the old folks well know, there were once two rival brothers who lived in castles on opposite banks of the Rhine River, waylaying travelers from their fortresses in the airy heights of the mountains. They had hardly done away with one another when their younger sisters inherited the opposing castles. As Mother Nature had intended, these two unfortunate creatures immediately decided that they would be enemies as well. It ran in the family.

The one sister "had a marvelous set of jugs," as a visiting Bavarian, who was rather less than refined, liked to call a full bosom. The other sister couldn't hold her own up there, but had gorgeous, long legs. Somewhat unrefined herself, she called her sister's rather chubby legs "clubs you could use to squash eels in the Rhine." She took lessons on the frivolous Zeedijk in Amsterdam in how to dangle pretty legs out of a window with the greatest effect, so that even the already-satisfied men, the ones least willing to pay, would be guaranteed to wind up between them. The other sister just hung her jugs out of her window in the castle. To put it bluntly, the rivalry between the two blonds was in full swing and even attracted people from the Outre-Rhin with anti-German sentiments, such that the coffers of the two ladies of the castles rattled with gilded silver and a few unwillingly given wedding rings. Things could have cheerfully gone on like this forever, except for the fact that all things on this earth must come to an end.

This end came for both of them in a lamentable fashion. A certain Sir Bluebeard, whose beard was actually rather more red than blue, was entrapped in the legs of the less be-jugged of the two sisters. Unfortunately, he hadn't brought any silver, only lust, and this incensed the little blond bitch, who came at him with scissors. He became enraged and did her in. He loaded the uncompensated corpse onto his steed with the strange name of Granny and galloped straightaway to his own Castle Redbeard in the resinous woods of a neighboring mountain. The other sister watched all of this, not without some goodwill, and from that day forward she doubled her horizontal income, thinking her competition to have been eliminated. She wantonly spent a large amount of gold on some obscure Nibelungen hoard.

A woman from St. Goarshausen, who was already ancient at the time and is now the only living eyewitness, told me that another blond in the vicinity of the now-deserted castle stole the show with the following trick: She always combed her golden hair high above on a protruding rock when the blessing rays of the sinking sun had just reached those peaks, and its blazing light combined miraculously with the forsythia-yellow glow of her floor-length hair to form a veritable glitter and gleam. The dusky, twinkling shimmer, always just before sunset, blinded the johns, who came in low rowboats rather than on high horses. In droves they fell victim to the witch, as the surviving sister dubbed her. The woman constantly combing away at her hair took her victims for every penny. The mouth of the woman watching from the other bank fell open so far in astonishment that her absolute envy filled her mouth, and she forgot to breathe. She was done for right away. All that remains of her and the blue-red—bearded robbery victim is legend and the ruins of two once-proud castles high above the Rhine. The wind blowing over the Rhine howls in the barren windows of bleak, overgrown rubble of walls.

However, our now-toothless wise woman tells us that the lady with the golden comb is still playing the temptress up there on the high rock—who knows for how long—still skimming off from the lovers of gold, even though the competition in the setting sun has long been a thing of the past. However, tales tell us that she had the foresight not to entrust her high-karat Rhine gold to the caverns of the Nibelungen below the flow of the Rhine. A forward-thinking woman, she instead secured her future by depositing it in Deutsche Bank in the legend-poor city of Frankfurt.

Every 25 years, out of pure thankfulness, the employees of Deutsche Bank take a steamer trip down the Rhine, interest rates permitting, and, while singing the bank's official anthem ("Money makes the world go 'round/Money lost and money found/We rich all hearken to the sound"), pay proper homage to the tale-filled rocky landscape. Then, hooting and hollering, drunk on song and the phrase "I don't know what all this means!" the bankers also notice the castles of "Two Spiteful Sisters," which seem to glow in the evening light. But then the employees retire to the wine cellar in vine-covered Rüdesheim to quench their thirst (perhaps for more fairytale gold).

Even today, you can sometimes see a shimmer from the legendary rock in the Rhine, and you could almost believe that you hear ghostly laughter coming from jaws with glittering teeth of pure gold, being hit over the head with a hint of pure gold. And no wonder: the art of goldsmithing of the Nibelungen gnomes and their descendants in the Rhine, below the Rhine, and around the Rhine has long been renowned the world over!

The reader whose senses have not been transfixed by the glimmer of so much gold is advised to read between the lines in Heinrich Heine (or in Erich Kästner: "No longer does anyone die on board a ship merely because some blond woman is constantly combing her hair").

# The Secret Mint in the Rock

For many long, sonorous years, an indeterminable tinkling, clinking, and jangling could be heard loud and clear whenever one traveled up or down the German Rhine. Later, although the rattling and metallic clatter grew softer, mysterious sounds could still be heard for an eternity after the first known records of ghostly sounds emitting from the cleft walls of the echoing rock. Until, at last, our oh-so-enlightened century finally did the ghost in.

Ghosts, perhaps, clattering around as they practice their trade? Leprechauns, maybe? Spirits that can be heard but never seen? That would be unearthly, fantastic, unthinkable in this day and age, and strictly forbidden. Therefore we are pleased to clear up the secret of the clinking and clanking on the Rhine.

Who solved the mystery of the clinking rattle on the Rhine? A cleaning lady from the pious, carnevalistic, gray but perpetually jovial city of Cologne. She was in the employ of one Professor Sudden, whose dwelling was far upstream from his office, near the looming rocks of the mid-Rhine mountains. Known as The Inspector, his Maruschka brought him onto the trail of an adventurous, profitable, and in no way fictitious summation.

Professor Sudden is a detective in the pay of the state. He lives for questions, seeking, and is well funded ferreting out things that are rather fishy. When his cleaning lady, her tongue perhaps rather loosened by delicious Rhine wine, allowed it to slip in her broken German that her second job, paid under the table, was "sweeping in de frront of a cave," it was quite natural for him to ask, "Where?"

"In best knowing, I can no say."

Coolly, he corrected her, "You mean, not to the best of my knowledge."

The stylish woman, who hardly looked Eastern European at all, replied, "Thees way or that, no matterrr. Tell you nossing, ees best for you. Nossing knowink, nossing worried, yes?"

"I'm not worried at all, Maruschka dear, but I am curious to know where the cave is. What is there in this neatly swept cave? Gold?" How on earth did that question come to him?

He looks at the lovely woman, this unknown girl who was recommended to him by an acquaintance, not without goodwill. He is even beset by lascivious thoughts as he regards her promising proportions and hums to himself Isolde's love and death song from Wagner's *Tristan und Isolde*. Who is his cleaning lady anyway? There is something secretive, almost dangerous even, in her being. He always makes sure that she is never alone in the house, now that he is a widower and the house is deserted when he goes to his office in Cologne. She doesn't answer the question about gold, and he digs deeper but casually, as though his questions were unimportant: "Maruschka, if you're sweeping in or in front of a cave, then people must live there, right? But that's none of my business."

Surprisingly, after another glass of the dry wine, she whispers a reply, "Rrich people. Very rrich man ... uh, much money, but I'm not knowink, I'm only sweebing metal."

This piques his curiosity, but he distracts her: "Well, thank you for all your hard work, Maruschka. You don't need to do the kitchen today since your bus isn't running because of the Catholic holiday and the flood. Two phenomena at the same time—that means nothing's open and nothing's running. So I'd be glad to drive you to your cave in the rocks, if you like."

She puts down her wine glass and puffs, "Grreat! In a Merrzedes! So heppy ... but hurry, please. Time is ..."

He marvels briefly at her funny-sounding rudimentary German, and then they are on their way. She insists that he let her out at a certain distance from the meeting place, and he pretends to drive away. But then he turns around and comes halfway back by way of a flood detour route. He just can't help himself; he spies on her.

He can just barely see her at the top of a switchback path, meeting a person who examines her carefully several times before both of them disappear into a cleft in the rock as tall as a house near an ancient chestnut tree. Strange, very strange, he thinks. All of his senses alert, he sneaks quietly after the two of them. The path appears to end at the chestnut tree, but it continues between two rows of blooming hawthorn bushes and leads directly into the darkness of a gap in the rock. Professor Sudden shivers in the cool of the shadows. Now he holds his breath; he can see an armed man standing behind a protrusion of the rock. Quickly, he ducks into the thorny undergrowth and stays there in breathless silence and suspense.

Coming from the rock in front of him, a clinking and sounds like metal being hammered can be heard, barely noticeable at first and then becoming increasingly louder. Professor Sudden is flabbergasted. It is pollen season, and our Inspector, allergic to any kind of impurity in the air, is desperately holding his itching nose shut. In vain! His sneeze resembles a miniature explosion!

Immediately, the man standing watch whistles a signal and leaps in the direction of the hiding place with his gun drawn. Almost lame from fright, our detective tries to crawl backward deeper into the underbrush when the ground beneath him gives way and a trap door opens, dropping him into bottomless depths. He lands hard and looks up in time to see the trap door close by itself about fifteen feet above him.

"Where am I?" the poor man asked himself as he picked himself up. In the semidarkness, he becomes aware of several light sources in the smooth rock walls and a spick-and-span stone floor. He is just barely able to duck behind an ancient metal chest when he hears his Maruschka's voice: "No, there's no one in here, and I didn't hear anything in the vault ... except ... just a sec, the trap door must have snapped shut. It was open to air it out. It must have been a rabbit or that stupid watchman out there. Moron." She is speaking perfect, accent-free German! The Inspector hears her leave with another person and ventures out of his hiding place.

From a neighboring, doorless, subterranean room, he hears a man ask his Maruschka, "What did you tell him about where you were going, you careless wench?" What Professor Sudden would have given to hear a name!

But his cleaning lady answered, "That's no kind of language for a public prosecutor! Don't worry; he doesn't know anything about all this here. I looked through his files— he's completely occupied with the bankruptcy of G. and has no clue about us at all."

"Good, Mariell, very good. You can go ahead and quit there; Sudden isn't any more use to us. He doesn't know our coin ... good." And he hears them both walking down an eternally long hallway interrupted by stairs.

From further away, the detective hears another voice: "It must've been an animal. Sorry, Boss."

The prosecutor makes himself heard: "Better a false alarm than a real one that comes too late. Well done, Sharpshoot, go back to your post." From then on, sounds could be heard that seemed to come from a foundry.

Professor Sudden's ears prick up when he hears the name. "But that's Sharpshoot from the G. Company! Goodness, what have I stumbled into? And my cleaning lady is a double agent spying on me for the public prosecutor. That could only be ... yes, it's him, the false factotum!"

Professor Sudden would prefer not to reveal how he was able to free himself from the trap in the rocks. However, once the famous prosecutor had been arrested, the robbers' lair had been excavated, and the treasure had been secured, he later testified in court that he listened to people counting gigantic sums of money. These were huge amounts of money that were being counted, not fictional ones at all! In the words of the Nibelungen Counterfeiters: "Five hundred thousand today, 300,000 yesterday plus tomorrow—that's 2.5 million for this week alone! The scam is coming along. We still need about 12 million more to pull down the entire red-light district in Cologne and realize our dream of a new financial tower of power. Brilliant, my golden boys!" This turned into a brilliant failure.

Maruschka, alias Mariell Doublette, emerged as the mistress of the boss of the Clang Gang and did her time in a comfortable prison with all the trimmings. The gang didn't get its name for a ghostly clanging, but rather for a very real clanging of the sorting machine in the mountain that sorted all of the falsely minted gold, silver, and jubilee coins, almost like one of Grimm's fairytales. The many credulous buyers didn't find out until the trial—thanks to The Inspector—that they'd been bilked and their supposed precious metals were actually false coins, lead with pretty paint on it. Oh, the poor little rich people!

Today, the subterranean passageways and rather luxurious rooms welcome refugees from the Balkans, where Maruschka is allegedly from. The machinery from an adit that hides an ingenious connection but was directly connected to the autobahn aboveground can now be admired in the German Museum in Munich, where the sky arches white and blue—not the reverse like in the rest of the world—over coins, counterfeiters, buyers, and believers in the supernatural, until the end of time.

What else could it have been, this enigmatic tinkling, clinging, and jangling, than counting money in coins? That even happens today, in other places. From six to seven, it was still child's play at first for the worshipers who had fallen victim to the Nibelungen myth, but when millions began to come, the game was soon up with the hocus-pocus, the subterranean goings-on at the dark streams flowing through the proud Rhine, which unrelentingly flow and surge around these obscure rocks, and occasionally are gilded in the beautiful sunset glow of forgetting.

But even so, at least as the new Miss St. Goar—the buxom, constantly plastered Wine Queen from the Year of Our Lord 1999—believes, the Rhine caves are haunted again. And how! Still, this time it's a few hundred kilometers upstream. Our friend Mariell, who has in the meantime been released for all-too-good behavior ("Ready for anything and anyone!" was her suggestive motto; she must have picked up from those good old goldless socialists from East Germany who went down on that philosophy themselves), landed in a Middle Eastern country that hadn't signed any international extradition treaties. After yet another change of identity and location, she is still living off the fat of the land in a small mountainous country—in other words, like someone who is dipping into an unknown well. These wells continue to merrily bubble along up in the Alps, where the blackest of affairs are gently covered by the whitest of snow, and at a profit at that. It's haunted up there, think the envious ones who don't see even a little bit of snow melting over the modern treasure caves of the Nibelungen, not even in high summer.

If that isn't fantastic and beautiful, like everything that we believe in too little or too much, believe in the power of gold. So keep listening for the clandestine rattling and jingling of metal everywhere, and don't go fishing alone in the muddy waters of the Upper Rhine because ... who knows!

P.S.: There's one more epilogue worth recording. Marlene Dubia, alias Maruschka, alias Mariell Doublette, became homesick and came back to the Rhineland. In an 8-star club, she failed to impress the new public prosecutor with "I bow beforre the divine in myself" even a little bit. He had her arrested, gave her castor oil, and a while later she played the golden goose. She positively jingled with nuggets of real gold that she had greedily swallowed in order to bring them into the country without paying tariffs. Fabulous stuff, that oil! Before Mariell's extradition, after six or seven days of custody, the generous state returned 97.5 % of the gold to her because that's just how the German fiscal laws are—praise and honor to whoever brings value to the land! No matter in what clever—or disgusting—manner.

For the rest, I, the narrator, am the only person in the entire curious world who truly and precisely knows where the legendary treasure of the Nibelungen is really located. But I won't betray that enigmatical location. And it is unwise to

157

follow me in my midnight wanderings along the Middle Rhine. I have always enjoyed misleading people. But perhaps I am misleading myself as well and must wait another few millennia until the Rhine has run dry and I can get out pre*cise*ly where my divining rod always kicks up, when I am deadly certain that the Loreley is watching, loafing about in her lofty heights. Her shining light blinds me, and I don't know anymore where I am, who I am, and why I'm writing all this down! Isn't that crazy?

# The Workers in the Dark

**B**onn, in days gone by. The poor government was bankrupt. It could see no way out, was hopelessly in debt, and declared itself unable to pay. The wolf at the door even caused the federal eagle on the flag to be brought inside; money could no longer be spared to run the wind machine that helped to simulate a proud and noble flapping in the wind. Illusions showing false things to be true were the order of the day; but the favorite type of illusion was self-delusion, which led to disillusionment.

Things had gotten so bad that the Minister of Finance—who, by the way, couldn't even count (according to the *Times*), since in the state where he was elected, it's a short path from altar boy to Minister—used up all of the income from taxes on repayment of debts. It wasn't a pretty situation. Furthermore, state spending for state pensions had grown to unpayable proportions because there were always more government employees who were constantly being voted in, voted out, and switched around. Thanks to the government's praiseworthy generosity, they all automatically became eligible for state pensions after three—count 'em, three—months in office. It was the hunt for government posts that kept Bonn alive. But why take and not steal?

Only a miracle could save the system from total disaster! Neither religious pilgrimages nor fervent prayers seemed to help much. What to do? Yes, what? "Let's sleep on it," sighed the good Chancellor. One evening, he placed his rusting collection box from forgotten times of crisis before the door of his high office and sat up in bed to wait out the calamity.

What a wonder! Overnight, the collection box was full to the brim! And with pure gold, which gleamed and glittered even in the Bonn fog. The portly Chancellor almost did a little dance. The next evening, he placed two larger pots in front of his door, and they were full on the next day too. Thereupon, he dared it with four, then eight, then sixteen, then thirty-two; he always put out twice as many as he had the night before in the cool, fogged flood plain of the Rhine until the otherwise cheerless street of the Chancellor had become a gigantic collection plate for alms of gleaming gold, with welcome results. Who was going begging to whom? Who was the helper in the dark?

Every morning at precisely 7:45, gold coins clattered in containers that were constantly larger and more numerous. The containers were produced round-the-clock by the comrades in East Germany, so that the national emergency would improve quickly and the economic doldrums would transform into a surplus.

"But," the Chancellor, who had never before been plagued by doubt, asked himself, "who could be behind this blessed influx of gold? It couldn't possibly be a gift from a fairy godmother or anything magical; no, here on the lower Rhine we're far too gray, no magic at all. Who or what is at work here?"

He persuaded his dutiful wife to stay awake with him one night and spy on the miracle, to investigate it thoroughly like good Germans. How they both marveled when they saw what happened in the depths of night: a giant horde of strange little people, in shabby work clothes, starving, unwashed, unrested, and all without the seal of a union on their clothing. At the stroke of midnight, they began diligently, selflessly, and without resting to turn a thing until it turned into a gold coin and fell gleaming into the waiting pots. This made the Chancellor suspicious, and his wife as well. "Working without pay and anonymously? What would happen to us if that got out? We must keep this a secret between us!" No sooner said than done. Behind closed doors, the first couple, who wanted to show their gratitude, discussed how these industrious little workers in the darkness could be rewarded for their unpaid acts of humanitarian aid.

He suggested setting up sausage stands; she recommended a night bar and a milk bar, plus a welfare station, all at no cost (in other words, at cost to the state). Both of them could already see how the honors would pile up in front of them for this economic miracle they were working.

The obscure new source of income ("This chancellor is a genius!") soon replaced the other, more common yet dried-up sources such as sales tax and income tax, payroll tax and payroll advance taxes, back taxes and union taxes, bribes and court costs, capital gains taxes and offset of expense offset, corporate taxes, inheritance taxes, write-off benefits, income from exploitation of position, value-added and no-value taxes, and "you name it" taxes. The amassing of money pleased the offices, officials, and office-weary; the corps of bureaucrats grew quickly since there was far too much to do and to spend. Overnight, the other statistics improved as well: the skyscraper-high backlog at the Ministry of Justice, the mountain-high pile of debt at the Ministry of Finance, the expired timetables at the Ministry of Transportation, and last but not least the fatal heaps of overproduction at the Ministry of Economics—all of these problems simply solved themselves. The most stunning development—the name says it all—was at the Ministry of Development, enveloped up to now in poorly developed processing procedures for overdeveloped and underdeveloped countries, developed by the left wing.

Finally, our government could again allow itself to support the farmers, who were starving, gnawing on their own tablecloths, to support them for producing too much and, in good bureaucratic language, to provide an orderly means for destruction of the mountains of European meat, butter, apples, tomatoes, cheese, and potatoes. This government aid created a curious cycle that was kept in motion because everyone profited from it. Except the taxpayer. First, a hefty injection of money for overproduction and then lovely subsidies for destroying the same subsidies; it all made perfect sense!

Yet another miracle occurred: for the first time since its inception, the Ministry of Defense was able to freeze an enormous amount of funds without threatening behavior coming from the east because (unfortunately) no new enemies presented themselves. Amazingly, no inquiries from crisis areas of Africa occurred, either. The market for weapons of mass destruction dried up. However, in military terms, the cool term "freeze" does not mean anything like "economizing." Oh, no. Weapons must still be produced even if they are not used! The ever-growing junk heap was truly a sight to behold.

In addition to all the surplus, there was also the discontinuation of the un-German cultural commission. There was simply no more culture to maintain because everyone was happier without culture.

All this peace, jubilation, nonsense, and free time naturally led to the fatty degeneration of the population of this land of milk and honey, who were constantly amusing themselves. They even celebrated outside of the thirty-six state-mandated holidays. Vacation canceled out vacation. The new German weekend began on Thursday and ended on Tuesday. One whole day remained for the workweek, but even that was too much for the unions, who wanted to cut it in half with a doubled compensation for lost wages! That was too much for a lot of independent companies. The result? Wednesday became the day to call in sick. For reasons of obesity. The Bible was rewritten: "But you are not in the spirit, but in the flesh!" Wonderful. The entertainment industry flourished, becoming the largest industry in all the land. New diversions were constantly being invented so that it wouldn't occur to anyone to look for any sort of meaning behind the whole thing. Some of the rosy-faced citizens differentiated themselves from actual swine only by virtue of being bipeds. A satisfied grunting that could be heard from a long way off was drowned out only by snoring in the middle of the day. People were too tired for sex, and so the rest of Europe noted with delight that the Germans were slowly dying out. Use of remedies to combat the results of the new, celebrated society of leisure was on the rise: remedies for too much fat, too many sweets, too much rest, too little exercise, too much sleeping in front of the television, too much of too-much-of-a-good-thing. Life in the Federal Republic became like a gigantic leeching.

How did it come to this? The caring wife of the Chancellor had something of a social conscience. She was less able to see the wonderful work of those working there in the darkness than the pure misery of the workers. So she suggested social improvements for services aboveground and belowground. There were the latest provision rights, housing aids, new naturalization rights (since many of these industrious workers spoke with foreign accents), union memberships, pensions and health care, and overtime regulations—who had to do what when and where (but not why). And tax-haven passports!

Then the workers in the dark had their springtime too. They stopped working when the union regulations said so. They threw their hammers down. Now sick days and vacation happened at night too. They took their cue from the people above. The clever reader will already have figured out how the circle is closing and how the people in the light and in the darkness are coming ever closer!

But this is no fairytale; this is a story from those days that is almost to be taken literally. And it doesn't end with "and they lived happily ever after," but rather with the completely different ending of the non-fairytale.

The global weather warmed up and changed the climate in the most radical manner possible. In central Europe as well. There was a long drought during which it was so dry that, for example, the general water consumption had to be regulated and, among other things, flushing toilets was only permitted for five minutes a day, which really stank. Everyone was left high and dry. A beer at Oktoberfest cost around three thousand marks. The result was a noticeable drop in the primal German urge to booze it up. Once everyone had jumped on the wagon in the heat, there were floods of biblical proportions, which flowed over the overeaters (who where now gobbling up a little less) and the drunken revelers at midnight, until 98.8% of the land was underwater. It was impossible to see the banks of the

Rhine; it stretched from Holland to Poland and devoured all the borders and tributaries, including the Weser, the Elbe, the Main, and the Oder. Everything went under in the Rhine. Even the water. It was so humid as to be unbearable. But no one at all thought of biblical floods; the people had long since abandoned all belief in a higher power and adored only manna and themselves. Manna didn't come. The oracle of Delphi occurred as a solution, and a delegation was sent to the south-southwest.

When the question was posed to the legendary oracle whether an improvement in the weather would be forthcoming, it prophesied darkly from the hole in the rock: "The owl coughs behind the mountain." This caused a terrible panic. The words of the oracle have been expertly translated from the ancient Greek in which they were spoken by an expert in the field, Dr. Heinrich Hahne. He was an admirer of fallen cultures, but he was reported to have smiled knowingly and somewhat laconically upon hearing the oracle's words. The oracle was not consulted any further because the debate in the Bundestag regarding the rather enigmatical answer began immediately and continues to this day, now that the drunken Bundestag has emerged from the waters after moving back to Prussia. Other unpleasant things have since surfaced out of the flood as well, but never the workers in the darkness. Thanks to their oversupplying, they had long since made themselves scarce, feathered their nests, and relocated. Who knows where they may turn up some night!

The ones at the top, or at least the ones who had gotten to dry land and had neither drowned nor died of thirst, sank in mire a meter deep. They found themselves very mired down indeed! The daydream of the land of milk and honey was gone, with or without the collection boxes. They say that a great darkness sank over the magical land. Supposedly it didn't happen all that long ago. And, as is so accurately said, "the government is still looking for a bright spot!"

They may have a long time to wait.

But, as every traveler knows, a different wind is blowing in Berlin, a fresher, freer, more Prussian and liberal one, a fairer one than in Bonn. And so the hope cannot ever be completely given up, the expectation of a moment of light.

# FROG TALES,
# 1945-1950 RETOLD

# 1

The blue morning of May 8, 1945 had barely cast its hope-filled glow over the still-smoking ruins of the Wuppertal Valley. The war had just ended. Young Fridolin, burning for action, sneaked out of the remains of his parents' house and wandered freely, looking for nothing. As so often happens, he who looks for nothing finds more than he who looks for something. Fridolin was attempting to leap over a puddle that had formed between two gruesomely gray ruins when midway in his jump a bright phosphorescence distracted him and he landed—splash!—in the middle of the puddle.

Defiant, he remained in the murky brown water, looking like a drenched poodle, seeking the light that caused his fall. He knew it wasn't an unexploded phosphorus bomb, a relic from the firestorm in the Year of Our Lord 1943. Wuppertal went up in phosphorous flames and entered the annals of the war in photo negatives. Alas, this irritating luminescence came from a pair of glowing eyes belonging to a frog—a talking frog.

"Pick me up, take me home with you," the frog said to Fridolin,

This was very strange, Fridolin thought. Unfortunately, he had not read any fairy tales about frogs since time out of mind; not even "The Frog Prince." He began to think rather slowly, as one is accustomed to doing in Wuppertal. A frog? In the middle of the ruins. One that can talk? Might this mean something? He paused for reflection. It must! A frog that can talk and has glistening green eyes couldn't possibly be from a fairy tale. There must be something significant behind it. So, Fridolin dared to question the frog.

"How come you can talk? You ain't nothing but a frog."

"Of course, I'm not a frog that can talk. I am an enchanted mountain princess. You need only take me with you to Barmen and you will witness a miracle!" This was followed by a gentle, "Please."

Poor befuddled Fridolin first thought, well, if this mountain princess is under a spell, I ought to help her. And Mom probably wouldn't mind this kind of frog.

"I'll take you home, but you must keep your mouth shut or I'll throw you in the river," he answered the frog.

No sooner said than done. With his fingers spread, he took the slimy frog with the green eyes from the puddle's filthy water and let it—or her—slide into his pants pocket.

Fridolin's home had neither gate nor door and no panes in its windows. He climbed into his "bedroom" through one of the holes in the wall. Mom didn't need to know that he was up and about so early. He lay down again in his bed, a halfway-comfortable mattress pile, and tried to go to sleep. Silence reigned for only a moment before the frog's voice sounded from his pocket:

"You must take me out and lay me in bed next to you. Otherwise the magic won't work."

Disgusted by the idea, Fridolin thought for a moment: should he or shouldn't he? The world is in chaos, Wuppertal is in ruins, and a talking frog with green eyes isn't something you find every day. Besides, I've never slept with a princess, but what if ...? He overcame his doubt and laid the frog carefully in the bed next to him. It had hardly turned into a beautiful, naked, rosy princess when the door opened and Fridolin's parents stormed into his room.

He quite innocently explained everything to them, but to this day neither his father nor his mother believes his frog story.

Back then; no one in Wuppertal had even the slightest patience for that sort of foul magic.

# 2

In short order, Fridolin's unbelieving parents kicked both him and his frog princess out of the house. Poor Fridolin was deprived of house and home. He sought and found shelter in Elberfeld beim Königsberg and spent a long, blissful day with the woman born of puddle foam until he fell asleep from an overwhelming, heavenly fatigue. He awoke alone. As darkness fell, the enchanted woman had taken to her heels leaving only a moist souvenir.

How sad that she's gone, he dreamed. Full of desire that threatened to burn him up at any moment, Fridolin got up and wandered aimlessly through the rubble of Wuppertal. He thought of the frog that had brought him an ambivalent, yet short, happiness as he passed beneath the overhead cable car tracks still cheerfully squeaking in spite of everything. He was amazed when he heard a frog's voice behind him. The frog was hopping in a puddle as if it were agitated.

"Take me with you! Take me with you!" the frog pleaded while looking at Fridolin with black frogeyes as big as saucers.

Fridolin eagerly picked up the little hopper and could hardly wait to get it to the ruins that were his temporary shelter. And? Nothing happened!

"Ain't you enchanted or something'?" Fridolin asked, disappointed.

"Oh, just let me sleep next to you and in the morning, you will see wondrous things!"

Thereupon the frog went to sleep, with gurgling snores. In his joyous anticipation, Fridolin was not able to sleep. But as the first rays of Wuppertal's gentle, gray sunlight fell, fatigue finally overtook him. Just then, the frog woke up and hopped around on Fridolin awakening him.

"What now?" Fridolin asked yawning.

The little frog's eyes flashed. "Come with me to the barren ruins. I'll tell you a secret."

And so it was that Fridolin wandered through the ruined landscape of Wuppertal with a frog in his pants pocket. As they passed a kiosk that sold lottery tickets as well as cigarettes, boiled potatoes, and skim milk, the frog suddenly screamed at the top of its lungs: "Bet! Bet!"

The kiosk owner leaned out. "Ya didn't need ta say it so loud, kid. Ya can see right there that I have a lottery office."

He was one of the early war profiteers who had set up his stand thanks to black market money and emergency aid from the transitional government that wanted to distract its starving populace with lottery games. The Kiosk owner had set up shop right where any wanderer through the ruins would be dreaming of luck and nothing else—a strategic location. When the frog started croaking "Bet! Bet!" again and Fridolin didn't open his mouth, the owner grinned.

"I suppose you're a ventriloquist or something'. Ya chose the wrong time; used ta be stuff like that drew a crowd," he said to Fridolin.

Unperturbed, Fridolin, who remembered the first frog, bought three lottery tickets with his very last pennies. He turned around, walked wearily "home," and fell asleep without giving another thought to the frog. Dreaming, he saw himself as a Croesus who would make the Wupper River navigable so he could sail in luxury down to the Rhine and, from there, upstream to the elegant Baden-Baden, where there were no ravages of war.

The next day he found out that he had actually won the big jackpot, thanks to his amphibious friend. He picked up the money and took the first train down the Rhine to beautiful, sheltered Baden-Baden, the meeting place of those who had remained safe and sound during the war. In Baden-Baden the preferred language was French.

That evening, full of joy, almost in a state of delirium, Fridolin went with his companion to the famous casino. It was foreign to him. He didn't dare sit down while he watched the playful casualness of the gamblers. The frog, which Fridolin had forbidden to yell, whispered to him from his pants pocket, "Roulette."

Perplexed, Fridolin sat down at a roulette table surrounded by the finest ladies with feather boas and other things that he had never before experienced. He truly didn't know up from down.

"Bet on red 13! Put everything on red 13, everything!" the frog said.

"Shut your little froggy trap," was what Fridolin wanted to say. Wuppertalers are not born gamblers and it is difficult to bring them out of their peace. But when the frog demanded even louder, "Put everything, everything on red 13!" Fridolin had had enough and fled from the casino.

"Are you crazy? You want me to blow everything I've won here?" He wanted to preach a sermon of prudence to the frog.

"You must bet everything on red 13, right away," the frog urgently pleaded with him. "Believe me! Just bet everything on red 13!"

Fridolin thought, okay, fine. This frog has already made a lot of money for me and if a frog from the Wuppertal ruins tells you to do something, you should probably do it. And he went back along the Seufzerallee into the casino.

He amazed the croupier and the entire classy company with his risky move. He took out the money he had sewn into the lining of his shabby suit and bet it—all of his winnings from the Wuppertal lottery—on red 13. The ball rolled. A tense silence filled the room. The roulette wheel spun, first quickly, then slower as the ball jumped from one field to another. Spellbound, Fridolin stared at red 13, while the other players watched the ball. The game will be over soon, and I'll go home a millionaire, he thought happily. But too soon, because the damn ball did jump into the red field and hopped from the 11 to the 12 to the 13, but then came to rest in red 14. Then he heard the frog's voice, which had picked up a few French croaks, coming out of his pocket, *"Merde, alors, merde!"* ("Crap, oh crap!").

Here, modesty requires your humble narrator to be silent about the rest. I will shy away from even mentioning the further graphic language that followed. But I will now cry a great big tear for Fridolin and his hapless friend, who he threw carelessly into the River Oos. After being thrown out of the casino in Baden-Baden (because of observations regarding the ventriloquist's suit) and the miserable hitchhike back to rubble-covered Wuppertal, we lose track of Fridolin. Maybe he is looking further up the Wupper for talkative frogs that are gifted with or without a feel for luck, but who do not have a propensity to use obscene language. But for that we would need a spinner of fairy tales, and you can only find them on the Internet, right?

A few years after the great defeat, the people of Wuppertal pulled themselves from the ruins (unjustly inflicted, in their opinion). At that time, every evening a fantastical, fairy-like shape, a dreamily beautiful young thing, haunted Wuppertal's fields of rubble. Many people believed "she ain't real," but stayed frozen in wonder, their mouths wide open when she appeared. Others observed that this stranger hovered rather than walked. Wasn't that odd? A wonder?

No wonder at all for the ghost watchers in the mountains who had also seen several other unearthly forms slinking through the windy Wupper Valley—"sect gorge and piety valley," in the words of Freiligrath. With their inner eye, or with some other sense known only to ghost lovers, they saw the second face.

Just another wondrous being, from some world other than our own, they thought. But from which world? Soon, word began to spread about a princess from another star. The rumor ran all the way into the deepest black-green Westerwald; where the wind whistles as cold as in a soldier's song, ice cold. What to do about that wind? Eucalyptus drops.

Even Fridolin heard of this wondrous creature. He was living rough-and-ready (well, more rough than ready) selling edible snails, chewing gum, truffles, and lean or fatty frog legs. He was also a storyteller. For example, he told of a time in far-away, elegant Baden-Baden, where he had gargantuan winnings at roulette with the aid of a magical betting partner. He turned the facts completely on their heads without blushing. Fridolin, the amphibian lover, now had a far more mature and manly air about himself, at least on the outside. He thought quickly, "Maybe there's something to it. I'll go take a gander at this rubble princess."

One man, one word. On his way back into ghostly Wuppertal, a mysterious, ancient woman met him on the western edge of the forest. She asked him, her hair pulled up under a blue scarf, where he was going.

Amused, Fridolin retorted, "What's that got to do with you, old Auntie?"

"I see you, poor fool, falling into the arms of a beautiful woman, a sorceress who climbed from the depths of the Wupper," the mysterious ancient responded. "Take heed of my warning, and mistrust her misdeed; or, foolish and young, you'll be tricked by her tongue."

Fridolin was now anxious and wanted to have a chat with the Auntie. He asked impudently, "How would you know about Wuppertal?" He turned back towards her, but the obscure apparition had disappeared behind him in the dark of the forest. Only a blue scarf, left hanging in the brush, remained as proof of her ghostly presence.

In the cool of the evening, the rather undernourished Fridolin suddenly grew cold. He shivered, was somewhat dazed, but continued stumbling along his undeviating path. He was not wandering at random; he had a clear goal. His steps became ever quicker in the rising cold of the autumn night. His thoughts flew to a possible romance with the sorceress of the Wupper.

Let's not begrudge him his short-lived dreams, even if we already sense something unpleasant in the very thought of the rubble princess. What was balm for his ailing soul is for us a huge warning sign. But who can keep him from continuing his downward path? Who can resist the force of this inexplicable attraction?

Arriving in Wuppertal at midnight, we see Fridolin heading for his parents' house, which is in better condition than when we saw it last. He is overcome with wonderment when, in spite of all expectations, he sees a female shape dipped in blue moonlight, wandering like some otherworldly thing through the night shadows.

"That must be her," Fridolin thinks. His heart beats more wildly. He isn't cold anymore; a fire runs through his limbs—

all of them. Only Fridolin and the apparition move through the street. It is as still as a graveyard. Fridolin approaches her. She turns to him with a smile so full of sweetness that his senses desert him entirely.

"Where shall we go?" she whispers, her beautiful face surrounded by a halo of otherworldly light (the like of which Fridolin has only seen in pictures of the Madonna).

He falls victim to her pining look: such a beauty, such a glow, and such a heart-rending loveliness. Fridolin is torn. He hardly feels her arm when he pulls her to him, then hesitates, blinks his eyes, and shakes his head. The dream seems all too blessed. He plucks up his courage: "Come to me!"

How wonderful are these beings in the night as they surrender to the blue moonlight.

Fridolin slows questioningly in front of his parents' renovated house, but this beautiful stranger pushes him gently through a new, unbarred side door into a darkened room, which, besides a window full of moonlight holds only a mattress. The blessed, cursed lovers lower themselves onto the mattress, and Fridolin stares unbelieving at his dream, his vision. She places a little golden crown in her glistening hair and now really looks like a fairy tale princess. In heaven's name, that can't be. But she breathes into his ear, "Come, kiss me. Don't be a frog!"

At those words, poor Fridolin jumps up as though a tarantula has bitten him, and, much to the horror of the beautiful woman, Fridolin screams.

"Help!"

Chaos ensues in the house, the lights turn on, and his parents come pounding down the stairs in flowing nightclothes. They burst into his room and cry, "Fridolin! You're back! Where were you? And what's that?" They point to a disappearing being made of blue light that glides through the open window and disappears. How painful it is for us when we are torn from the depths of our dreams before they have come into bloom.

"And what's that over there?"

Fridolin's parents point to the mattress next to him. A fat, blue-green frog with a golden spot on its forehead is sitting their ribbiting. Unbelievable, but true! Poor Fridolin stammers, "Mom, Dad, I must be crazy."

They comfort him. "No, no, you're not. At least it's just a frog this time and not some princess. But why?"

We are wondering the same thing. His dream is past, he's home at last. So now let's let him clear away the rubble of his Wuppertal imaginings (or ours).

***

Here comes a bird, flying towards me at an incredible speed. He lets a scrap of paper fall from his beak. I read: "Fridolin sends his greetings. He now lives in..." Unfortunately, the end of the paper had been nibbled away by the beak. Just before the bird flies away, I am quite sure that I can clearly see him raise the longest feather on his left wing up towards his head. What a smart aleck!

# About the Author

| | |
|---|---|
| 1939 | Born in Wuppertal, Germany |
| 1943-53 | Idyllic childhood in Miltenberg, Bavaria |
| 1957 | Preparatory school ("Gymnasium") in Wuppertal (last in Math and Latin, first in the Arts) |
| 1959 | Apprenticeship as an industrial textile designer (Dessinateur and Patroneur, Vorwerk & Co.), first drawings and paintings |
| 1960-62 | Studied at the School for Applied Arts, Offenbach and State Academy of Fine Arts, Karlsruhe, Germany |
| 1963 | Studied at the National School for Decorative Arts in Aubusson, France; assistant set designer, Germany |
| 1964-65 | Student of Jean Lurçat (1892-1966, the revivalist of modern tapestry) in Saint Céré, France |
| 1966-85 | Tapestry designer ("Cartonnier") for Aubusson and the Munich Gobelin Manufactory |
| 1986-present | Self-employed as an exhibition coordinator, designer of tapestries and handmade rugs, textile arts organizer, author of novels, theatrical sketches (performances in the U.S.), poetry (included in anthologies), translator, lecturer on medieval tapestry at universities and the Smithsonian Institution, creating large-scale drawings, art advisor, art dealer, and the most demanding job of all: parenting and bringing up children |